Fire Engines of North West England

Robert F. Bonner

Nostalgia Road Publications

Contents

The **Nostalgia Road** Series™

is produced under licence by

Nostalgia Road Publications Ltd.

Unit 6, Chancel Place

Shap Road Industrial Estate, Kendal LA9 6NZ

Tel. 01539 738832 - Fax: 01539 730075

designed and published by

Trans-Pennine Publishing Ltd.

PO Box 10, Appleby-in-Westmorland, Cumbria, CA16 6FA

Tel. 017683 51053 Fax. 017683 53558

e-mail: admin@transpenninepublishing.co.uk

and printed by

Kent Valley Colour Printers Ltd.

Kendal, Cumbria

01539 741344

Front Cover: *The classic 1960s fire engine at work in a typical northern street. This 1963 Dennis F24 pump ladder (XRJ 538) from Salford's Broughton sub-station, is seen in the Pendleton area of the city in September 1970.* Bob Bonner Snr.

Rear Cover Top: *Two contrasting scenes in the North West: this photograph depicts a Bedford J5/HCB water tender of Lancashire County Fire Brigade (289 LTD) dealing with a grass fire near rural Carnforth in July 1963.* Joe Hain

Rear Cover Bottom: *A Volvo FL6/Saxon water ladder of Greater Manchester (X851 KNA), which was still new when it found itself in the thick of the Oldham riots during May 2001, and visibly bears the scars of a "stoning" attack between the cab windows.*

Title Page: *The scene at Paulden's department store, Cavendish Street, Manchester on 8th September 1957, showing a 1935 Dennis Light 6 pump with John Morris bodywork. The blaze ultimately required 20 pumps and five turntable ladders from several North West brigades.* GMFS Museum

This Page: *A unique fire appliance, the first motor fire engine in Britain! This 'modern' unit went to the Borough of Eccles on 8th September 1901, and would be the only fire appliance ever built by the Protector Lamp and Lighting Company.*

ISBN 1 903016 38 X

British Cataloguing in Publication Data

A catalogue record for this book is available from the British Library

Above: *A marvellous photograph from the 1930s depicting several Leyland appliances from North West fire brigades gathered together for an unrecorded event, possibly one of the rallies organised by the Lancashire Fire Brigades Friendly Society. In the foreground, a 1925 Leyland FE (TD 3473) of Darwen Fire Brigade, converted to pneumatic tyres, followed by the 1936 Leyland Cub* "Hamer" *(BTB 870) of Rawtenstall.* Arthur Collier

Introduction

For many, the North West region was well known for its proliferation of separate, urban fire brigades, principally in the textile towns of East Lancashire, but also around Merseyside and other coastal areas. Many of these smaller authorities were often completely surrounded by the larger county brigades, but special relationships and the interaction between the various brigades helped shape the service in this region. Consequently, it was not unusual to see fire engines from five or six different brigades tackling one large incident in the region; yet they were independent too and each brigade had their own design features or allegiance to one particular manufacturer.

Interestingly, the region is inextricably linked to some of the most significant events in the development of the fire service and its equipment. Manchester for instance is credited with organising the first truly municipal fire service in England in 1826, whilst in 1831 the first steam fire engine to be bought by any brigade went to Liverpool.

This steam appliance was delivered by Messrs. Braithwaite & Ericsson only a year after the famous steam railway locomotive trials at nearby Rainhill, where the same manufacturers had exhibited their *Novelty* engine; it is said that the technical specification of this locomotive owed much to the company's earlier experiments with fire engines.

The country's earliest motorised fire engines appeared in this region at the turn of the 20th-Century and such diverse landmarks as the first British-built turntable ladder and the first appliance with a blue flashing light were also noted in the North West. Yet the region's early "fire engine establishments", administered by the primitive local authorities of the 18th- and 19th- centuries, were provided with simple manually-operated pumps, usually horse-drawn. These were often of local manufacture, the various town's commissioners either not trusting those made in London or else wishing to avoid expensive delivery charges.

In the years following the industrial revolution, in which the North West played such an important part, many engineers and scientists were to be found in the region with the skills to build fire pumps and equipment. Although few examples of such machines survive today, manual appliances by such obscure makers as Barton or Hollins can be found in local museums.

Other northern companies, founded by personalities from fire service backgrounds (such as William Rose or John Morris), were much more prolific. These two particular firms soon began to challenge the bigger London manufacturers of Shand Mason and Merryweather, and both were soon to become serious contenders in the world market. The Rose Company even produced its own steam fire engines between 1897 and 1902 whilst Morris was to remain a major player throughout the motor era. In the post war years, the area has continued to be associated with fire engine manufacture and remains full of interest for the enthusiast.

The tough and extremely varied operational environment found in the North West has produced a wealth of innovative and specialised fire appliance designs often initiated by the brigades themselves, often through pioneering partnerships between fire authorities and manufacturers. Although such developments have generally taken place in the larger cities such as Liverpool or Manchester, innovative designs and applications have also appeared (and continue to do so) in brigades like Lancashire and Cumbria, many of which also appear in the book. Some North West fire brigades became adept at building their own vehicles, albeit in relatively small numbers, and examples of these are also illustrated.

In a book of this size it would be impossible to provide a detailed fleet history of every brigade in the North West, but I have attempted to give a flavour. All those in operation between 1948 and 1974 are represented, as are the five new authorities serving the region today. The different types of appliances preferred by each are discussed and the more significant or unusual vehicles are illustrated.

Robert F. Bonner, Rochdale, July 2003

Below: *A typical large fire scene in the Lancashire cotton spinning belt; this fascinating scene at Rake Bridge Mill, Rochdale in 1956 shows vehicles attending from at least four separate authorities in the North West. From the left is ABU 980, a 1938 Leyland Cub limousine pump of Oldham, AEN 402, a Fordson 10-cwt van of Bury (probably bringing a relief crew), OTJ 491 Commer/Cuerden water tender of Lancashire County Fire Brigade dating from 1951, an unidentified open appliance, possibly a Dennis, and Rochdale's 1954 Bedford S-Type emergency tender with HCB bodywork.* Clifford Ashton

Pre-War Appliances

The first motor appliances to appear in the North West were placed in service almost simultaneously at Eccles and Liverpool, although they would only have short working lives. Together though, both these appliances played a very significant part in the development of the fire engine as they were the earliest motors to be operated by any British fire brigade.

It was in September 1901 that the Borough of Eccles, four miles to the west of Manchester, purchased a *"motor car capable of carrying five men and the necessary fire extinguishing appliances to render first aid at a fire"* from the Protector Lamp & Lighting Co. Ltd. in the town. The company was better known for the manufacture of miners' lamps, but also produced a small motorcar called the "Bijou", on which this experimental fire engine was based.

Above: *The first self-propelled steam fire engine for any British brigade was this 300-gpm Merryweather "Motor Fire King" delivered to Leyland UDC in 1903. Apart from a sizeable fleet in Liverpool, few examples of this type of appliance were actually operated in the North West. As might be expected, the Brigade chose a Leyland motor pump for the steamer's replacement.* Lancashire Libraries

The 7-hp vehicle cost £180 and came with a one-year maintenance contract from Protector. Fully laden with crew and equipment it was capable of speeds up to a breathtaking 14mph! This was obviously quite fast enough for Eccles, because within a few months of delivery it met with an accident in the Town's Yard. During a driving lesson the new machine collided with an iron pillar; but this later resulted in a complaint from the makers when it was decided to repair the damage without informing them!

Top Left: *Liverpool's early motor appliance fleet included two of these electrically-powered Cedes pump escapes with Simonis fire equipment, the second is shown here in 1909. A Magirus turntable ladder had been supplied by the same firm two years earlier.* Jack Robertson Collection – FBS North West

Centre Left: *The first example of John Morris' famous turbine motor pump, constructed on the Manchester-made Belsize chassis (EN 187), and delivered to Bury Fire Brigade in October 1910. Previous Belsize-Morris appliances had been fitted with chemical first-aid apparatus only. Three years later the machine suffered a mishap when it rolled down an incline and landed on its side in a water-filled pit. When recovered two days later it was found to be undamaged!* Andy Bentley

Bottom Left: *Oldham's first two motors were by Argyll of Scotland, not a particularly common make but one who produced several fire engines in their attractive factory just south of Loch Lomond. Neither was fitted with a pump, being classed simply as "motor tender." The second is seen here when new in 1910. Subsequently registered BU 250, the machine was named* Grime, *not as a reflection on the mill town's environmental state, but in honour of a local dignitary.* GMFS Museum

Meanwhile the Liverpool Fire Brigade was also experimenting with motor propulsion, having arranged a trial by the local Daimler agent, The Royal Carrying Company. The latter mounted a fire tender body onto a Daimler, somewhat larger than that of the Eccles appliance and for fire fighting, a 60-gallon "chemical engine" was fitted to the vehicle. Testing took place during August 1901 following which the Watch Committee agreed to purchase the appliance.

However, after further trials it was decided that the Daimler was not suitable for operational use and it was converted to a runabout. Despite such inauspicious beginnings (the Eccles engine also proved unsuccessful) the region can nevertheless claim to have had the first motors in the British fire service.

The North West had yet another important "first" in 1903 when the newly-constituted fire brigade at Leyland in Lancashire took delivery of a self-propelled steam fire engine. Known as a "Fire King," the Merryweather machine had previously been sold to overseas customers only, but the Leyland example was the first of its type in the UK. By this time, more reliable motor engines had begun to appear, commencing with the Merryweather appliances supplied to Tottenham and Finchley in the London area in 1903 and 1904 respectively.

From that time, more and more motors were built and by 1909 it was clear who the major contenders in the market place were going to be. As well as Merryweather & Sons of Greenwich, John Morris & Sons Ltd of Salford, Dennis Bros. of Guildford and Leyland Motors in Lancashire soon established themselves in this specialised field and would spend the next 30 years in serious competition with one another. Whilst Merryweather and Morris both had long histories in the fire equipment trade, the other two had more of a road transport background but each quickly earned a high reputation for quality fire engines.

Despite the failures in Liverpool and Eccles, other fire brigades in the region were not slow to take on the new technology and appliances from all of the four main builders soon began appearing in North West fire stations. Among the earliest brigades to buy "proper" motor appliances were Rochdale (Merryweather 1908), Birkenhead (Dennis 1909) and Bury (Morris 1910) who all took this step before their larger neighbours Manchester and the 'once-bitten, twice-shy' Liverpool. The Bury machine was the first of John Morris & Sons' well-known Belsize-chassised models to have a main pump, driven by power-take-off, previous versions having "first-aid" equipment only.

The Belsize, available in either 4- or 6-cylinder format, was a solidly built, chain-driven motor which proved to be a good basis for fire engine work. Large numbers were supplied with Morris bodywork and escape ladders to brigades world-wide, the largest single fleet probably being that of Manchester Fire Brigade who purchased eleven between 1911 and 1920. The company soon began to offer the German Magirus turntable ladder assembled at its Salford factory, and they remained the UK concessionaire until the 1950s. (It should be noted that this fire engine company had no connection with Morris cars or Morris-Commercial lorries).

Leyland's first motor pump was supplied to Dublin in 1909 but from that time until World War II, after which the company bowed out of the general fire engine market, a great many North West fire brigades would remain faithful to the Lancashire product. Although attracted by the undisputed quality, the fact that they were locally-built must have appealed to many authorities. German-made turntable ladders, in this case by Carl Metz, were also assembled and marketed by Leyland. The first two production models, supplied in 1924, were of wooden construction with a ladder length of 85ft and went to Manchester and Wigan respectively. Further north, Barrow-in-Furness was another early user of motors, opting for the Merryweather Hatfield pump as already supplied to both Rochdale and Salford

Top Right: *The first motor engine to reach Cumberland was this 50hp chain-driven Merryweather with 350-gpm Hatfield pump delivered to Workington in 1913. On 24th September 1913, whilst still brand new, it attended a serious farm fire at Lamplugh, nine miles away, working successfully for 21 hours.* GMFS Museum

Centre Right: *In the 1920s, few fire engines could match the clean, refined lines of a Leyland, as exemplified by this 1921 model FE of Horwich UDC (TB 7832). The town received frequent assistance from the private fire brigade at the Lancashire & Yorkshire Railway Company's locomotive works, and shared its chief officer. The Leyland was even housed in a fire station within the works.* Arthur Collier

Bottom Right: *Macclesfield in Cheshire had two fire services, one run by the council and a separate, volunteer brigade. The latter purchased this Ford BB tender in 1933 (ALG 884) with bodywork by Locomotors of Macclesfield, part of the Hovis group. Although having no fixed pump, two Anzani 150-gpm trailer pumps – detachable from their own wheels – were carried. Almost 60 years later, the same firm built a batch of water tenders for Cheshire Fire Brigade, but in a different factory.* Roy Breese

Despite having a reciprocating piston pump, as opposed to the more efficient turbine design, the 'Hatfield' was a popular choice for many newly motorised brigades. It was named after one of the firm's prestigious customers, the Marquis of Salisbury of Hatfield, Herts. The Barrow machine was delivered by rail to Lancaster, then driven the rest of the way. Powered by a 4-cylinder 60bhp Aster engine, it could pump 450-gpm of water, as was publicly demonstrated at the Town Hall on 17th November 1911 when a jet of water 160 feet high was supplied from an underground tank in Cavendish Square. Prior to the display, the machine was christened *Catherine E. Butler.* The idea of naming new appliances, usually after local dignitaries, dated back to the horse-drawn era and was especially prevalent in this region; Blackburn retained the system until disbandment in 1974. Another Merryweather Hatfield became the first motor fire engine to reach Cumberland when it was commissioned by Workington Fire Brigade in 1913. This example was supplied via a local dealer, S.T. Croasdell & Co.

Prior to World War II, the North West was covered by around 200 separate brigades, the standard of which varied widely. At the upper end were the highly-disciplined and professional police brigades that operated in the larger towns and cities such as Burnley, Liverpool and Manchester. Next came the municipal brigades, administered through a committee and often with a mixture of whole-time and part-time staff, though generally quite efficient, and below these came the less affluent units which were completely retained (part-time) or even volunteer-crewed. By the 1920s all but the smallest had become at least partly motorised.

At this stage, appliances were still built with the open (or Braidwood) style of bodywork, where the crew hung on for dear life every time they turned out; accidents were not infrequent. Safer layouts in the 1930s, such as the all-seater "Transverse" or "New World" designs and even completely enclosed machines, seemed slow to catch on in this region! A notable early exception was the 1934 Albion-Merryweather limousine appliance supplied to Lancaster Fire Brigade, in which the crew travelled in comparative comfort. Not far away, Blackpool also embraced the limousine concept, purchasing several Leyland examples from 1936. By the end of the 1930s examples of just about every make of fire engine could be found in the region, with many chassis, bodies, pumps or ladders being locally-built.

Top Left: *One of the last wooden 85ft Metz ladders, by now fitted to the later Leyland TLM chassis (KF 6683), was supplied to Liverpool in 1931. After a long working life, it was acquired by the Metz Museum in Germany in 1963.* Jack Robertson Collection – FBS North West

Centre Left: *A Dennis/John Morris pump of Burnley Fire Brigade dating from around 1930. Carrying a 30ft Ajax extension ladder and – unusually for an urban brigade – a spare wheel, it sports the Salford manufacturer's classic gold-lined livery of the period.* GMFS Museum

Bottom Left: *Often considered to have been the prototype for the Dinky Toys "streamline fire engine," this limousine with 275-gpm Hatfield pump was supplied to Lancaster in 1934. Although TJ 7561 was actually based on an Albion, it was Merryweather's policy to keep the chassis builder anonymous wherever possible.*

Above: *A splendid view of the former Barrow-in-Furness fire station on Abbey Road, taken about 1938. The fleet is representative of many local authority brigades serving industrial towns in the period just before World War II. Flanked by a pair of Austin ambulances we see (l. to r.) a 1937 Fordson V8 tender (EO 6908), a 1937 Leyland-Metz 90ft turntable ladder pump (EO 7012) and a 1919 Dennis Braidwood pump (EO 1656).* North West Evening Mail

Right: *This handsome Leyland FT4 limousine pump, seen outside the old Tithebarn Street fire station in Preston, was one of an identical pair supplied to that local authority in 1939. Although a vast improvement on the open "Braidwood" style, this design was slow to catch on, not least because it could not carry a wheeled escape. The outbreak of war, and the introduction of utility appliances, effectively halted the progress of this design.*

Above: *Auxiliary Fire Service personnel muster on Salford fire station yard prior to setting off for Liverpool to assist with that city's air raids in December 1940. The Ford lorries represent the larger type of towing vehicles acquired by brigades in the early part of the war; many travelled great distances under regional mobilisations of this kind.* GMFS Museum

World War II and The National Fire Service

As the threat of war loomed at the end of the 1930s, the region's fire brigades realised that, with its docks, oil installations, shipyards and heavy industry, the North West could expect to be a prime target for enemy air raids. The Home Office began to supply emergency fire appliances from about 1939, and whilst some areas were fortunate enough to receive self-propelled Bedford and Fordson fire pumps, the bulk of the issue was trailer-drawn, presenting brigades with the problem of finding sufficient towing vehicles.

In Liverpool, the Salvage Corps fitted towing hitches to its fleet in order to help the city if required. Elsewhere, various cars and light lorries were pressed into service, many of them already past their best. When fully laden with five or six firemen, hose, brassware, ladders, and pulling a heavy trailer pump, they were usually working far beyond their designed capabilities. Because of this, large American cars such as Chryslers and Buicks became a popular choice.

The Fire Brigades Act of 1938, which required every local authority to make effective arrangements for fire protection, was followed by the formation of many new fire authorities, some of which were very well-equipped. Wirral Fire Brigade, for instance, began operating from 1939 with a new Leyland pump escape, a Bedford tender, a trailer pump and an ambulance.

The two small towns of Stretford and Urmston, within whose boundaries lay Trafford Park and part of the Manchester Docks, decided to join forces and organise a professional brigade with a fleet of modern appliances. Therefore 1939 saw the delivery of two Dennis/John Morris pump escapes, a Leyland Cub pump, a Leyland-Metz 104ft turntable and a Leyland emergency tender, all with the impressive consecutive registrations ETC 1 to 5. Other new brigades, operated by Rural District Councils, provided fire cover to a number of small towns in the same area.

Not all authorities were able to get their hands on the new equipment. One noticeable effect of the hostilities was the non-availability of the German Magirus and Metz turntable ladders as sold by Dennis and Leyland. The Leyland-Metz for Stretford was one of the last two made, whilst similar appliances ordered by Blackpool and Blackburn had to be cancelled. Blackpool's chassis was already built, so the brigade accepted Leyland's offer to build a limousine pump body instead.

Warrington advertised for a new TL in 1939 but this never materialised either. The Home Office then released a number of new turntable ladders on a ‘grant basis’; all were built by Merryweather (the only *British* ladder manufacturer) on either Dennis or Leyland chassis. Under this scheme, Liverpool, Birkenhead, Salford and Manchester all received new Leyland-Merryweather machines in 1940. The latter (GNC 800) was damaged during a Blitz attack just two weeks after being delivered. Between August 1940 and May 1941 the areas of Manchester, Salford, Stretford, Liverpool, Wirral and Barrow all suffered sustained bombardment, which in turn strained the local brigades to their limits and showed up the shortcomings of the mixed fleets very quickly.

There were insufficient towing vehicles and the ex-regular machines were hardly designed for blitz fire fighting. Features such as the small water tanks (typically 40- to 60-gallons) soon proved inadequate. Appliances were sent great distances to assist other areas, but on arrival it was often found that the hose couplings from one brigade would not fit those of another.

The experiences of Britain’s fire service during the Blitz led the Government to merge all 1,400 pre-war regular brigades – and all Auxiliary Fire Service units – into the National Fire Service, with effect from 18th August 1941. The country was divided into regions, with Manchester chosen as the headquarters for the North West (No.10) Region. This was sub-divided into four Fire Force Areas, based in Liverpool, Manchester, Bolton and Preston. A later reorganisation introduced additional area headquarters at Warrington, Stalybridge and Kendal.

One of the first tasks for the NFS was to renew the appliance fleet. The blitz had already taken a toll, with several machines being either destroyed or damaged. The most pressing need, that of reliable towing vehicles, was resolved with the introduction of the Austin K2 auxiliary towing vehicle (or ATV). Other new appliances issued to the NFS would include heavy and extra-heavy pumping units, escape carriers, and various special appliances such as canteen vehicles and breakdown lorries.

Top Right*: Some AFS units had to make do with whatever towing vehicles they could get hold of; for example The Kendal Auxiliary Fire Service is seen here at Rinkfield with their Coventry-Climax trailer pump attached to a Bedford W-type lorry belonging to the local firm of S. Downham & Son.* Margaret Duff Collection

Centre Right: *A typical AFS unit comprising of a converted Ford saloon and Standard-Gwynne trailer pump. Many such combinations were operated by AFS crews before the nationalisation of 1941 led to the issue of purpose-built towing vehicles. The Blackpool-registered vehicle is photographed in an Emergency Repair Centre probably alongside the LMS Railway at Bispham’, note the carefully stacked railway sleepers and stores material ready to ‘instantly’ repair any bomb damage to the railway infrastructure.* GMFS Museum

Bottom Right: *A splendid shot of an ex-regular Manchester Fire Brigade pump escape wearing NFS livery. Here we see a 1937 Dennis Big 6 (DVU 785), in the Piccadilly area, which was cleared after the devastation caused by the “Christmas Blitz” of December 1940.* GMFS Museum

Particularly welcome in the heavily raided towns and cities were the new Merryweather turntable ladders on Austin, Dennis, Leyland Beaver and Leyland TD7 chassis. These were issued to those areas needing additional resources, or where particularly old ladders were still in service such as Bootle and Bolton, both of which had wooden apparatus from the 1920s. Blackburn's long-awaited new ladder, a diesel-engined Beaver (GXA 64), finally arrived in 1943, whilst Carlisle, Warrington and St. Helens also received their first turntables courtesy of the National Fire Service.

Thankfully the NFS and its new appliances never saw the level of enemy action for which they were intended, at least not on the scale seen in the twelve months prior to its formation. The NFS was disbanded on 1st April 1948 and the fire service handed back to local authority control. However, only the larger municipalities would be allowed to operate a fire brigade, and small rural or urban council brigades would merge into county control.

In the North West this meant 22 "county boroughs", the rest of the region being covered by new county council fire brigades in Cumberland, Westmorland, Lancashire and Cheshire. All had to provide the best fire cover they could, despite only having pre-war appliances (many of which were now worn out) and ex-NFS vehicles (few of which were really suitable for peace-time work).

A significant problem facing all municipal services at this time was the parlous state of finances in Britain, given the crippling war-debt that had to be paid. Substantial parts of the country still needed repair to war damaged property or infrastructure, and that which hadn't been damaged was largely worn out by six years of total war, in which period maintenance, spares and man-power had been in extremely limited supply. At the same time, Britain's motor manufacturers were given the order 'Export Or Die', as it was considered vital to concentrate production on overseas orders to gain much-needed American dollars. Therefore few commercial chassis were available in the period from 1945 to 1948, and full relaxation only came in the early 1950s.

With new appliances in short supply as a consequence, a great deal of ingenuity was shown in adapting, or even completely rebuilding former NFS machines for their new role.

Top Left: *One of a number of 100ft. Merryweather turntable ladders on Leyland TD7 bus chassis to serve the region, GLW 417 is seen in its later, peace-time livery at Liverpool's Longmoor Lane fire station, Fazakerley.* Jack Robertson collection – FBS North West

Centre Left: *In a scene that could have been taken during the Blitz, a Fordson 7V self-propelled pump makes its way along the dock road in Liverpool, with the Overhead Railway visible in the background. In fact, GLM 659 was photographed whilst serving with the city's Auxiliary Fire Service after the war.* Jack Robertson collection – FBS North West

Bottom Left: *Looking immaculate in its "demob" livery of red with gold lining, this ex-National Fire Service Austin pump escape of Oldham Fire Brigade is still very much in its original condition, including the Barton front-mounted pump and Home Office-type escape. GXA 791 was later sold to the Ferodo works fire brigade in Derbyshire.* GMFS Museum

Above: *A wonderful scene from the 1950s as Barrow's 1937 Leyland-Metz turntable ladder begins its attack on a fire at the Cavendish Furniture Company, Duke Street in 1956. Parked behind is one of the brigade's unique Commer/Coutts appliances of 1952.* North West Evening Mail

BARROW-IN-FURNESS, CARLISLE, CUMBERLAND & WESTMORLAND (1948-1974)

In 1948, when the fire service was handed back to local control, almost half of the North West region became the responsibility of just two rural fire authorities. These were the counties of Cumberland and Westmorland, with headquarters at Carlisle and Kendal respectively. Additionally, the City of Carlisle (the only borough brigade in the two counties) had its own fire service meaning that there were two completely separate fire headquarters in the 'Border City' until Cumberland moved its base to Cockermouth.

A further county borough brigade was to be found at Barrow-in-Furness, south-west of Lake Windermere. This was actually in Lancashire, but was closer to Lakeland, a fact recognised in 1974 when it was absorbed into the new county of Cumbria. (It should be noted that the term county borough was used within the fire service regardless of any city status held, as at Carlisle). The fire brigades in Carlisle, Barrow and Westmorland were all combined with the ambulance services, a situation shared with three other North West authorities.

As may be expected in an area that included the more remote parts of the region, the majority of county fire stations were of part-time (or retained) status. In Westmorland, Kendal was the only station manned round-the-clock, whilst just three out of eighteen Cumberland stations were classed as whole-time, including the industrial towns of Workington and Whitehaven on the coast of the Irish Sea. In the north of the county, a total of about 90 square miles of Cumberland's area was protected by appliances from Carlisle by special agreement.

New fire appliances were in short supply in the early years of de-nationalisation, the earliest post-war deliveries being a Dennis F12 pump escape for Carlisle in 1952 and a pair of interesting Commers at Barrow the same year, both bodied literally "round the corner" by the long-established coachbuilder J.Coutts & Co. Ltd.

Top Left: *Cumberland shared the same problems as most other newly-formed brigades in the provision of new appliances, due to the limited availability of chassis and the overall cost. One option was to rebuild old NFS stock as seen in this rather poor (but rare) picture of a water tender mounted on a former Austin K5 'Mobile Kitchen' dating from the 1940s. The new bodywork, built by Cumberland Coachwork Ltd of Distington in 1950 to the brigade's specification, was reported as having "a correct place for everything and everything in its correct place."*

Centre Left: *This Simon pump/hydraulic platform was supplied to Cumberland in 1972 for service at Workington. Based on a Ford D1617 chassis, with an HCB-Angus body, the 50ft platform was the only aerial appliance of any description to serve in the brigade. HCB-Angus Archive*

Bottom Left: *After some post-war Dennis purchases, the City of Carlisle Fire Brigade turned to Bedford, commencing with this HCB-bodied water tender in 1960. The appliance, which survived until after the 1974 amalgamation, appears to have the full range of past-and-present warning devices, including bell, siren and two-tone horns, as well as a blue beacon and the original amber twin flashers.*

The Barrow Commers were given the 'special" registration marks, AEO 2 and 3 (but AEO 1 was kept for the Mayor's car!). In the shires, the rolling stock was rather more basic. By 1949, Westmorland had just three major pumping appliances across the whole county, along with five water tenders (almost certainly all of wartime design) plus some 18 trailer pumps. Trailers also accounted for more than half of Cumberland's pumping strength at this time.

Both brigades took steps to improve some of their ex-National Fire Service vehicles by fitting new or rebuilt bodies, thereby producing some very individual-looking appliances in the process. Additionally there were a number of hose reel tenders, adapted from wartime Austin auxiliary towing vehicles by the inclusion of a small water tank and reel.

Special appliances were few and far between with only the two borough brigades operating turntable ladders. Barrow's pre-war 90ft Leyland-Metz still had plenty of life left in it, while Carlisle had an even younger model, also on the shorter side, in the form of an 85ft wartime-issue Dennis-Merryweather. No turntable ladders or other full-height aerial appliances were ever operated by either Westmorland or Cumberland throughout the lives of either brigade.

Rebuilding of the vehicle fleets continued during the 1950s and 1960s, with the ubiquitous (and economic) Bedford chassis finding favour in all four authorities. Most of these were built by Hampshire Car Bodies, but Alfred Miles bodies could be found in Barrow, including an emergency tender of 1960.

The counties also liked Rootes Group products, with examples of both the Karrier Gamecock and its bigger brothers from Commer; particularly in Cumberland who bought virtually nothing else in the years 1960-70. Many of the water tenders in this brigade were specified with larger tanks of 500-galls or more, a reflection on the remoteness of some of the rural territory covered.

This feature was no doubt influential in the unusual disposal of a 1959 Commer/Carmichael foam/water tender to the Manchester Airport Fire Brigade in 1966, where its 900-gallon tank would be particularly useful for supplying the larger tenders out on the airfield. By then the turntable ladders of Barrow and Carlisle were ready for replacement, with both brigades opting for the Birmingham-built Haydon-Magirus 100ft model. A Rolls Royce-engined Dennis F37 was the basis for the Barrow machine. Yet Carlisle (perhaps influenced by near neighbours South West Scotland who already owned two similar Rootes Group vehicles) chose a Commer, which became the only turntable from this maker in the North West.

This deceptively beautiful part of the country is home to some of the most hazardous main roads in Britain, particularly the higher stretches of the A6 trunk route with the notorious Shap Fell. The completion of the M6 motorway in 1970 opened up the region to more visitors and increased the number of road traffic accidents attended by local fire stations, especially during the harsh Cumbrian winters. The often narrow roads meant that smaller, specialised rescue appliances would be the most appropriate for the purpose. Carlisle acquired a long-wheelbase Ford Transit rescue tender in 1973, whilst at Kendal (in Westmorland), a Commer Walk-Thru van was fitted with a range of pneumatic and hydraulic rescue equipment. In Cumberland, two Land-Rovers served the same purpose. A somewhat unexpected type of appliance for Cumberland was a 1972 Ford D1617/Simon 50ft pump-hydraulic platform with HCB-Angus coachwork for Workington; a similar machine on a Dennis F108 was the last to be purchased by Barrow Fire Brigade.

The latest front-line appliances for both the Westmorland and Cumberland fleets, before their 1974 amalgamation as Cumbria Fire Service, were all Ford but with an unusual bodybuilder winning the Cumberland contract. This builder was Gloster Saro Ltd, part of the Hawker Siddeley group who were better known for their specialised airport fire appliances. They did make a brief foray into the normal fire engine field, including the pair of water tender ladders supplied to Cumberland in 1973.

Top Right: *Westmorland Fire Brigade operated a number of Carmichael-bodied Karrier Gamecock water tenders, including this 1960 appliance (GJM 447), formerly at Kirkby Lonsdale and now preserved in the Manchester area*

Centre Right: *The increase in road traffic accident work during the 1960s, partly due to new motorways such as the M6, led many brigades to develop specialised rescue tenders like this 1967 Westmorland appliance at Kendal. Based on a 2-ton Commer Walk-Thru fitted with air compressor and pneumatic cutting tools, this type of vehicle was sometimes known as an "air van". The plain red livery would be considered inadequate for present-day motorway work*

Bottom Right: *Looking resplendent in its new paintwork, this 1969 Bedford TK with HCB-Angus water tender escape body of Barrow-in-Furness was unusual in carrying the 1952-vintage registration mark AEO 2, which was transferred from an earlier Commer appliance. It is seen outside the fire station on Abbey Road.* North West Evening Mail

Blackpool, Preston & Southport (1948-1974)

Three of Lancashire's borough brigades were clustered around the River Ribble, where the contrasting seaside resorts of vibrant Blackpool and gentile Southport flank the wide estuary leading to the once-busy inland port at Preston. The largest of these resorts is Blackpool, on the Fylde coast, whose most interesting period was undoubtedly the late 1930s when a fleet of innovative new Leylands attracted much professional interest.

One 1936 pump escape to a completely new design, was described as "semi-limousine" with sweeping roofline, enclosed seating, but no cab doors. Further stylish appliances over the next few years included some by H. V. Burlingham, Blackpool's famous coachbuilder, distinguished by having the brigade's name in separate chrome letters along each side.

Two ex-NFS turntables were replaced in the 1960s by a Bedford TK and an AEC Mercury, both with Merryweather equipment. Another Mercury that followed later was the only one in the region to have HCB-Angus bodywork, but the greater part of the post-war stock was Bedford. One peculiarity was a 1960 Bedford TK with outwardly normal, water tender-style bodywork by HCB but which functioned as a combined pump and salvage tender. In this role it replaced the famous Leyland limousine built on a 1939 turntable ladder chassis.

The life risk in Blackpool during the summer months was (and still is) phenomenal and to ensure adequate rescue capability a 70ft ERF/HCB-Angus/Simon Snorkel platform was acquired in 1972. Following a trend prevalent at the time, it was fitted with a pump and hose reel equipment, unlike an otherwise identical combination purchased by Preston that year. Two water tenders in 1971 and 1973 completed Blackpool's ERF fleet.

The ERF range had been introduced to the fire service at the 1966 conference of the Institution of Fire Engineers at Southport, its advanced engineering and new safety features making it a worthy addition to the long line of excellent fire appliances built in the North West.

Top Left: *Blackpool set new standards in 1936 with the introduction of the "semi-limousine" style seen here. However, Leyland No.4 (FV 6446), pictured at Lytham Road station, dates from 1935 and originally had Braidwood open bodywork. That appliance body was replaced in 1952 with this "look-alike" enclosed body by local firm W.T. Plant Ltd, costing £665.* Joe Hain

Centre Left: *The only Ergomatic-cabbed AEC/HCB-Angus combination to serve in the region was Blackpool's 1969 water escape (MFR 164G), which carried a 50ft metal escape. The somewhat shapelier roofline, as compared to the Merryweather version, is clearly seen in this view.* Brian Edwards

Bottom Left: *One of four Alfred Miles-built emergency tenders to operate in the region, this short-wheelbase version of Preston Fire Brigade was exhibited at the Chief Fire Officers' conference in 1957. The metal-framed body, featuring Miles' characteristic triangular grill, completely hides any clues to the precise type of chassis, but its Bedford manufacture is identifiable by the badge on the front.* Joe Hain

Southport operated one of the region's joint fire and ambulance services and covered an area twice that of Blackpool's. It was, however, operationally quieter so the fleet was more modest. A 1961 Dennis F28 pump, having the usual trim appearance associated with that series, and a 1954 Dennis F12 pump escape were the main workhorses until the arrival of a Liverpool-pattern 50ft Dennis-Simon pump/hydraulic platform in 1971. The F12 was notable for its unusual "Beware Fire Engines Following" sign beneath the rear number plate, no doubt to alert any hapless holidaymakers who found themselves trapped between it and the F28!

An attractive Bedford TK emergency salvage tender with Carmichael body and a 1961 AEC/Merryweather turntable made up the borough's front-line fleet. The latter was specified with a two-man cab, instead of the larger variety found on most others of this Marque. Considering that (at most fire stations) such appliances are normally only crewed by two anyway, Southport was probably the only brigade to get it right.

Southport gave names to its fire engines but, in a pleasant departure from the usual (if somewhat dull) watch committee dignitaries, chose more fanciful names like *Samaritan*, *Salamander* and *Salvor*. As a tribute to a fireman killed in a tragic fall from an earlier Leyland-Metz ladder, the Merryweather delivered in 1961 was christened *The Maurice Evans*.

Preston was principally a Dennis fleet after the war, apart from its own AEC/Merryweather turntable and a couple of "specials" on Bedford chassis. The latter included a 1957 emergency/salvage/hose reel tender, based on the J-Type chassis. Bodybuilders Alfred Miles of Gloucester, with their characteristic ingenuity, somehow managed to squeeze all the necessary equipment, including a tank, hose reels, ladders and portable pump onto the short wheelbase chassis, which gave 17 years of service to the town.

The other Bedford was a Pyrene foam tender, built in 1964 on a TK chassis. It incorporated a 400-gallon foam tank, along with 100-galls of water, enabling some 4,800-gallons per minute of "finished foam" to be produced. Such man-sized foam tenders were not particularly numerous in the borough brigades. The brigade's final delivery was a full-size emergency tender in 1974, based on a Perkins-engined Dennis F108. This appliance was shortly amalgamated into the Lancashire County fleet as part of reorganisation later that year, so it saw hardly any service whilst wearing the borough's 'Proud Preston' crest.

Top Right: *The Dennis F24 was favoured by a number of brigades, all of whom seemed impressed by its performance and functionality. This water tender version of Preston (PCK 999) dates from 1961.* Chris Heaps

Centre Right: *Southport Fire Brigade's Fordson 7V emergency/salvage tender (GJJ 33) was originally a heavy pumping unit of c1941, but it was rebuilt by the Corporation Transport Department in the 1950s. The roofline and lower panels betray its former profile.* Bob Bonner Snr

Bottom Right: *Manchester Road, Southport with (from right to left) Dennis F12 pump escape (JWM 266), Bedford TK/Carmichael salvage tender (BWM 602 B), Dennis F28 water tender (VFY 119), the unusual single-cabbed AEC/Merryweather 100ft turntable ladder (OWM 261) and a Daimler DC27 ambulance.* Jack Robertson collection – FBS North West

Lancashire (1948-74)

Although the County Palatine of Lancaster was one of the larger counties of England, the fire brigade only covered about two thirds of the area. This was due to the numerous county borough brigades, 17 in all, that existed within its boundaries, the largest such concentration in the British fire service. The brigade's 63 stations (in 1948) were thus responsible for all the portions in between. More peculiarly, the brigade covered Furness, a part of Lancashire but physically separated from the rest of the county, and having one of those county boroughs (Barrow) within its confines. The fire risk ranged from remote rural scenery on the edge of the Lake District, to mill towns such as Accrington and Ashton-under-Lyne. It also included Trafford Park, Seaforth docks and the seaside resort of Morecambe.

Above: *A fire at the former Warwick cotton mill in Middleton is attended by two Bedford water tender escapes - one an HCB-bodied J4, the other a Carmichael-built TK – and a Merryweather Marksman water tender on Ford chassis. Also visible are an 85ft HCB-Angus/Simon Snorkel, featuring the ERF "back-to-back" cab, and a pair of Bedford TKs (a canteen van and a control unit), both with bodies by Craven-Homalloy.* Clifford Ashton

Like most new brigades after the National Fire Service, Lancashire inherited a legacy of appliances of variable quality. Fortunately a number of the constituent brigades had been large enough to run decent fleets with some, such as Stretford and Morecambe, even having their own turntable ladders before the war. For this reason Lancashire never acquired any of the NFS Merryweathers found elsewhere.

Nevertheless, the first new appliance delivered to the brigade, in 1949, was a magnificent normal-control AEC/Merryweather 100ft TL (KTF 847), which was posted to Ashton-under-Lyne; it was quickly followed by another (LTF 716) for Accrington. Three Dennis F7/F12 and six AEC/Merryweather pump escapes were received around the same time. These were very much "city-type" machines, which never seemed at home in Lancashire; indeed three of the AECs were actually sold to Manchester Fire Brigade for its reserve fleet in 1963.

After this foray the brigade soon settled on the Rootes Group's Commer chassis as the basis for its pumping fleet (and certain special appliances). All were bodied by Blackburn-based Cuerden Motors Ltd. An unusual vehicle at this time was a smart emergency tender by Cuerden on a Commer Avenger coach chassis, stationed at Stretford. Modernisation continued apace through the 1950s, with a fleet of Karrier Gamecocks (also from Rootes). However in the 1960s the brigade moved up the range to standardise on the Bedford TK for a while, the first batch of these were built by a new name in the world of fire engines - Busmar.

This firm had evolved from the old Swallow Sidecars company and used the same Blackpool factory to build both fire appliances and ambulances for Lancashire County Council. The Busmars had the same unpainted aluminium finish and jack-knife doors as the brigade's previous appliances but with slightly roomier GRP cabs, giving a distinctive, modern style. Later on, the brigade returned to HCB-Angus for a sizeable batch of water tender escapes but to Lancashire's own design, which clearly mimicked the seaside product. Other Bedfords appeared in the guise of emergency tenders, control units and even turntable ladders.

Many authorities were cautiously trying out the new Snorkel platforms by Simon during the 1960s; Lancashire was no exception but its ERF-based 65ft model delivered in 1967 was unique! This appliance was fitted, at the brigade's behest, with an interesting crew cab comprising two standard ERF fire engine cabs joined back-to-back; the idea was so successful that it was later taken up by the manufacturers. With the dawn of a new decade the brigade transferred its loyalties to Ford. Fourteen of the turbo-charged D600 model, fitted with Merryweather's new "Marksman" body, made their entrance in 1970 and Ford's tilt cab must have been a welcome sight to Lancashire County mechanics schooled on the Bedford fleet. By now, the brigade had adopted a striking fluorescent livery dubbed "rocket red", that was introduced by Chief Officer Peter Darby in 1969 after trials in his previous authority of Nottinghamshire.

More Fords followed, mainly by HCB-Angus, and these served the county for the rest of the period covered by this chapter. As one of the largest Ford customers, Lancashire put them to good use in a variety of roles. As well as the usual water tender and dual-purpose appliances, two hose laying lorries, a Carmichael-bodied foam tender and an 85ft hydraulic platform were among the applications.

One special example was KTD 615K, a D1617 of 1971 with modified HCB-Angus bodywork. This was fitted with Simon's revolutionary new "Simonitor" equipment. As the joint prototype of the 1970s phenomenon, KTD 615K was exhibited far and wide, including a twin-town visit to West Germany, a long way from the cotton mills of Chadderton where it would spend its working life.

Above: *The classic good looks of the Cuerden bodywork are well illustrated in this shot of PTJ 840, a 1953 Commer 45A pump escape at Ulverston in the Furness district. An alloy extension ladder is carried in addition to the 50ft Merryweather steel escape, Cuerden were responsible for six curvaceous escape-carrying appliances and a larger batch of squarer, but nonetheless handsome, water tenders.* J.Wadsworth

Below: *Apart from one other for Warrington, Lancashire's eleven Busmar-bodied appliances were the only examples sold. Three operated from Accrington station, including ATB 235A, a 6-ton Bedford TK from 1963. During the 1960s, Lancashire had become synonymous with Bedford products, starting with the lightweight 4- and 5-ton TJ series, bodied to Hampshire Car Bodies' "cheap and cheerful" specification.* Joe Hain

Bury, Oldham & Rochdale (1948-1974)

To the casual visitor, it would probably be quite difficult at first to spot the difference between these south east Lancashire mill towns, nestling in the foothills of the Pennines to the north east of Manchester, but all three had their own separate identity. The trained ear might even detect a subtle difference between the Lancashire accents spoken in each. All three consisted (at one time) of acres of terraced houses, in cobbled streets, surrounding huge cotton mills in the region's spinning belt. Those same mills, now mostly disappeared, were responsible over the years for a great many large fires and plenty of smaller, though difficult and smoky incidents too.

The proximity of these fire brigades to each other meant that they inevitably worked closely together and shared many similarities. All were early converts to motor appliances, acquiring their first examples between 1908 and 1910, though of different makes. The pre-war appliance fleets developed along parallel lines, but whereas Oldham was a supporter of John Morris products, Rochdale and Bury were largely Leyland customers. Bury had, however, been the first recipient of the well-known Morris-Belsize motor turbine pump, which had been introduced in 1910. In the 1930s, the three brigades all purchased virtually identical Leyland-Metz all-steel turntable ladders within twelve months of each other.

Above: *An excellent view of the complete Rochdale Fire Brigade fleet taken about 1957. Prominent is the 125ft Dennis-Metz turntable ladder, flanked by two Dennis pump escapes, a pair of Bedford S-Type appliances (Miles water tender and HCB emergency tender), and a line of AFS "Green Goddess" pumps. The staff cars include the Chief Officer's Wolseley 6/90 and two Vauxhalls.* Clifford Ashton

After the war, separate policies were pursued with regard to appliances, and all of them operated what could be described as fairly mixed fleets; AEC, Albion, Bedford, Dennis, ERF, Ford and Land-Rover products were all chosen at different periods. Oldham and Rochdale started their post-war fleets off with the ubiquitous Dennis F7 and F12 models, together buying a total of four pump escapes between 1950 and 1953.

All were maintained in immaculate condition, averaging some 20 years' service each. Oldham's 1953 example (JBU 510) was one of only two F12s to reach the new Greater Manchester fleet in 1974. Bury on the other hand, went for an AEC Regent/Merryweather pump escape in 1950 and found it to give equally good value.

Despite all three authorities being separated by stretches of Lancashire County Fire Brigade area, with county stations in between, close liaisons were built up. Rochdale and Bury, for instance, had a mutual assistance arrangement whereby a standby pump would be sent by either brigade should the other be stripped of fire cover, despite that appliance having to pass through the Heywood (Lancashire) station area on its way, and therefore being hardly the nearest! As well as this very specific sort of agreement, all three brigades were used to giving assistance to (and receiving it from) the county service at large incidents. Additionally, the concentration of special appliances in one area, particularly aerial equipment, meant the boroughs were often called upon to help at Lancashire County's larger jobs. Oldham, with the highest number of cotton mills, had manned two turntable ladders after its 1935 Leyland-Metz was joined by a 1941 Dennis-Merryweather, courtesy of the NFS. These two elderly machines – each with green-painted ladders – saw plenty of active service and both happily survived into preservation.

In 1957, Rochdale Fire Brigade replaced its 1934 Leyland-Metz turntable ladder with something special. Despite the decline of the spinning industry in the 1950s the borough still had a great many cotton mills, perhaps not so many as Oldham, but they included the country's largest spinning mill which produced tyre cord for the Dunlop company. The new appliance (PDK 717) was a Dennis F21 with an unusual 5-section, 125ft Metz DL37 ladder, one of only two of this height in the UK; the other entering service in Belfast. Unfortunately the machine was unable to prevent the Dunlop mill from burning down three years later. This appliance is now also preserved and can be found in the Greater Manchester Fire Service Museum at Rochdale.

Another interesting Rochdale appliance was 5937 DK, which appeared in 1963, and was the prototype of Dennis' F36 model, famous for its all-round disc brakes. Oldham and Bury each chose the 100ft Haydon-Magirus turntable ladder when replacing their pre-war Leylands. Both were mounted on Dennis F-series chassis, but Bury opted for the less-common F107 version with the AEC diesel power unit.

Top Right: *The London-pattern AEC Regent pump escape, produced by Merryweather, was not particularly well known in the region, with only three brigades opting for this model. After being delivered to Bury in 1950, BEN 114 was christened* Aspinall *and gave over 20 years of service to the borough. The bus-style lettering on the crew cab door says "John Heap, Chief Officer."* Merryweather

Centre Right: *In this part of the world only the Bury Fire Brigade chose the lightweight metal-framed version of the Hampshire Car Bodies (HCB) water tender, which was distinguished by its stylish cab design. This type of compact fire engine was not usually favoured by the county boroughs, who generally went for somewhat heftier products. Nevertheless HEN 999, a Bedford 5-ton TJ-Type, still looks in pristine condition in this 1967 view, some eight years after delivery.*

Bottom Right: *The prototype for the new Dennis F36 range was this water ladder for Rochdale (5937 DK) in 1963, with Rolls-Royce engine and single-piece windscreen. The jack-knife doors and roller shutters were optional. Rochdale was an early user of the 45ft alloy extension ladder, but many North West brigades stuck firmly to the wheeled escape at this period.* J. Wadsworth

Above: *Appliances by Alfred Miles Ltd of Gloucester were not particularly numerous in the North West, but the County Borough of Oldham operated two. This 1959 water tender, based on a Bedford TD-Type (RBU 999), was followed by an emergency salvage tender the following year. The stowage for the Coventry-Climax portable pump is clearly shown in this photograph taken at Ascroft Street Fire Station soon after delivery.* Oldham Chronicle

Below: *One of several Haydon-Magirus turntable ladders to serve in the North West, this Dennis F37 (ABU 756B) was bought by Oldham in 1964 to replace its 1935 Leyland-Metz. It saw plenty of action at large mill fires in south east Lancashire, ending its days with the Greater Manchester Fire Service. In common with most Oldham machines, it showed some economy in the sign-writing department.* Oldham Chronicle

In 1968 George Henry Moore was appointed Chief Fire Officer of Rochdale and within a couple of years he had changed the appearance of the brigade's appliances. The first step was to paint all the front cab doors white, with the word "FIRE" written in black. In an area where the traditional red liveries had always prevailed (no yellow appliances were seen around here!), the new scheme looked quite attractive and gave improved visibility at night. It was one of the few non-standard liveries to be found in this very traditional region.'!

In fact, in view of its success, the white paintwork was very soon extended to incorporate all the front panelwork, giving Rochdale its own distinctive style. When CFO Moore moved to Sunderland Fire Brigade in 1971 he took the new livery with him and began to apply it to the Wearside fleet.

That same year Rochdale acquired its first ERF appliance (SDK 999J), which was an 84PF Perkins-engined model with HCB-Angus standard water tender bodywork. This was soon followed by a second ERF water tender and later an emergency salvage tender; all three had the same make of body and the extremely smart appearance of the brigade's red and white colours.

The three brigades followed the stereotypical "county borough" fleet pattern for many years, with two or three pumps, turntable ladder and emergency tender line-ups (although Rochdale once ran a separate salvage tender as well). It was not until the 1970s that the first signs of change could be detected. In 1971 Oldham replaced its wartime Merryweather turntable with a 70ft Simon Snorkel on an ERF chassis (fitted with Jennings coachwork, a 500-gpm pump and a 200-gallon water tank), which became the first hydraulic platform in this corner of Lancashire. The following year, Bury departed from tradition when it placed a dual-purpose, 50ft pump-hydraulic platform in service, again on ERF chassis and bodied by ERF Fire Engineering.

Rochdale, for its part, commissioned a Land-Rover pump in 1973 to the new generation "first-strike" design, built by Arnolds (Branbridges) Ltd. With special low-height bodywork and a front bumper-mounted water tank, this new appliance was another 'sign of the times' as it was specially designed to deal with fires in the planned town-centre re-development area, in particular the proposed multi-storey car park. As a matter of fact, the Land-Rover never operated as Rochdale had intended, as it was ultimately posted elsewhere by the new Greater Manchester Fire Service before the centre was completed, and did its most useful work at fires on the town's rubbish tip.

Although this book does not really cover the many ancillary vehicles attached to fire brigades, it would be a pity not to mention two very unusual examples operated by the brigades in this chapter.

For example, the local authority at Bury was probably the only fire service in Britain to operate a three-wheel Reliant van (HEN 88), while Oldham shared a similar distinction by operating a 1962 tipping lorry (998 CBU). The latter, a Bedford TJ, was a replacement for a wartime Austin, the function of which was to carry boiler coke to the borough's rather ancient fire stations. However, one can only wonder what the local inhabitants thought a tipper, laden with fuel, might actually be doing as it passed down the road in full fire service livery!

Bootle & Liverpool (1948-1974)

The two adjoining fire authorities of Bootle and Liverpool were amongst the great maritime brigades of Britain, thanks to a long, shared history of fighting fires in ships and dockside properties. Two major fires in the Bootle docks – Gladstone Dock Shed in 1949 and the *Empress of Canada* in 1953 – necessitated reinforcing moves across the region. Yet, despite the similarities of tradition and working practices, appliances in the two brigades had far less in common with each other.

Dealing with them alphabetically, it is worth mentioning that the two Merseyside brigades were quite different and Bootle's post-war fleet was principally made up of various Dennis and Commer models. The latter included a water tender and emergency tender, both with Alfred Miles bodywork. Two deliveries of particular note were a 1957 Bedford SL (long wheelbase S-Type) with a Morris-Magirus turntable ladder, one of only two in the North West, and a Swedish-designed Carmichael-Wibe "Orbitor" platform, with a working height of 72ft, dating from 1970. An interesting feature of Bootle appliances was their unusual, though attractive, signwriting in a flowing, script style.

After operating the country's largest steam fire engine (the 1800-gpm "Holt" of 1899), Liverpool's motorised fleet was launched in 1901 with the ill-fated Daimler described in an earlier chapter. This was followed by a number of self-propelled Merryweather "Motor Fire King" steamers and some interesting electrical-powered appliances by Cedes.

The bulk of Liverpool's modern appliances were from Dennis, with a sizeable batch of 1950s F12s being followed by an even larger one of automatic-gearbox F24s; the latter being highly successful and well-suited to the terrain. Later Dennis models – including the F34 and the "70mph" F44 – had an in-built foam-producing capability. Dennis "specials" included a 1954 Metz turntable, a control unit and a pair of London-style, long-wheelbase emergency tenders. As might be expected in a major riparian brigade, Liverpool once operated its own fireboat to protect the many parts of the dock areas only accessible by boat.

Top Right: *A variety of Dennis models were commissioned by Bootle Fire Brigade between 1949 and 1972, including this short wheelbase F35 pump escape seen at the Strand Road headquarters. This 1967 appliance carries a Merryweather 50ft steel escape and a short extension ladder.* Joe Hain

Centre Right: *European manufacturers still had some way to go before being accepted by British fire chiefs when Bootle purchased this 72ft Swedish-designed "Orbitor" platform in 1970. In this shot, taken soon after delivery, the well-proportioned lines of the low-cab Dennis F119 are nicely set off by Bootle's unique style of lettering.*

Bottom Right: *For many years Liverpool's fleet of Dennis F24 pumps and pump escapes were almost as familiar a sight as the Mersey ferries themselves and, undoubtedly, a "fireman's favourite". Some 24 were supplied between 1959 and 1963 including 1783 KC, one of five dating from 1962, and seen at Derby Lane station in the Old Swan district.*

The 300-ton Liverpool fireboat *William Gregson* had originally been supplied to the Belfast Harbour Co. in 1937 as the *Duchess of Abercorn* but was re-named and converted to a fire-fighting vessel in 1949. In 1963, the fireboat service was discontinued due to rising costs and the vessel was duly exported to start a new life in Africa. That year, Liverpool made a major contribution in the development of hydraulic platform appliances by becoming the first in England to commission a Simon Snorkel. Mounted on a new type of Dennis chassis, the machine quickly found favour in the city's busy operational environment.

The credibility afforded by such a reputable brigade helped to encourage the acceptance of platforms by the British fire service, and the LFB devised various standard drills and procedures that were later adopted nationally. A second Dennis Snorkel arrived in 1967. Later, the brigade promoted the use of the 50ft pump-hydraulic platform combination appliance. Four Simon PHPs (two ERF and two Dennis) were purchased by Liverpool and saw heavy usage at some of the country's busiest stations.

At this period Liverpool was one of the most progressive brigades in the country. Developments such as the "Green Wave" traffic light system, which provided a safe route for appliances through the city centre, kept the brigade constantly ahead. In contrast, the city was the last in Britain to use street fire alarms. In 1966, it became the first brigade to operate articulated fire appliances when five semi-trailers were purchased second-hand from a local brewery. The trailers, fitted with Scammell automatic couplings, were converted in-house into heavy-duty units for ship fire-fighting, bulk foam and hose transport and as a canteen van.

Two new tractor units were procured for this unique fleet that from 1969, were all housed in the spacious appliance room at the new Bankhall fire station. From the 1960s, the brigade was also responsible for fire cover at Speke Airport, the airport fire station sharing the same site as the local Banks Road fire station.

In yet another pioneering move in 1971, the brigade acquired one of two joint-prototype "Simonitor" appliances, built by Simon Engineering on (in Liverpool's case) a Dennis F49 chassis. This vehicle, again combined with a normal pumping appliance, featured a remote control monitor on an extending boom with no cage, but was never as successful as the PHP.

Top Left: *Liverpool acquired the first "demountable" fire engine fleet when it commissioned five of these Hands semi-trailers, and two articulated units, in the mid-1960s. Here JKD 121 D, an Austin FFK240 12-ton tractor unit dating from 1966, is shown attached to the bulk foam trailer, loaded with 1,000-galls of compound and associated foam-making equipment. The other unit, acquired two years later, was an Austin 1200FJT.* Liverpool Fire Brigade

Bottom Left: *The first hydraulic platform appliance in England was this 65ft Simon Snorkel delivered to Liverpool in 1963. It was mounted on a diesel-powered Dennis F117 chassis of radical design, with bus-style, drop-frame forward extension, permitting a low overall height and excellent driving position. Seen at a typical city warehouse fire, 9750 KF presents an extremely handsome appearance even by today's standards.* Simon Engineering Ltd.

Above: *This Dennis Big 6 pump escape (GNB 217), formerly of Manchester Fire Brigade, was photographed outside the city's town hall in Albert Square, soon after being completely restored by members of the Greater Manchester Fire Service Museum in Rochdale. The appliance was delivered in April 1940, originally serving at London Road fire station. After a new Gardner 6LW diesel engine was fitted in 1958, the appliance finished its service as a reserve and training machine*.

Right: *Seen outside Marsden Road fire station is Bolton's emergency tender appliance (FYH 85), based on a former Home Office self-propelled pumping unit of 1939. The vehicle had been completely re-bodied in 1952 by local coachbuilder Bellhouse, Hartwell & Co. Ltd. to this attractive limousine design. A very similar rebuild on a Bedford from the same batch could be found in nearby Blackburn.* GMFS Museum

Above: *Although North West fire brigades were not especially keen on non-traditional liveries, the next three illustrations depict some notable exceptions. Wallasey Fire Brigade's 1958 Dennis F24 water tender (FHF 60) attracts the attention of local residents whilst attending a fire in the town. The brigade was the only one in the region to experiment with the once-fashionable overall yellow livery, which was applied in the early 1970s.* John Murray

Left: *St. Helens was famous for its striking white and red appliances represented by this Leyland Beaver water ladder. Three similar machines – bodied separately by Carmichael, Woodward and Cocker – were purchased between 1971 and 1973.* Jack Robertson collection – FBS North West

Above: *In yet another 1970s livery style,* one of *Rochdale's two identical ERF/HCB-Angus water tender ladders is seen dealing with a fire in a row of derelict houses. SDK 999J was delivered in 1971, the white and red livery having been tried on other members of the fleet the previous year. The second ERF arrived in 1972 along with an emergency tender/control unit by the same chassis and bodybuilders*. Joe Hain

Right: *Bought to protect the major industrial and chemical risks in the South Wirral area, Cheshire Fire Brigade's bulk foam tanker began its career in the haulage industry. The 1969 ERF 68GX (NKF 470F) was purchased in 1979 from Yates' of Ellesmere Port, and converted into this smart 3,000-gall foam carrier for the local fire station. The classic good looks of the ERF, with its LV-series cab, seem well suited to a fire service livery.* Bob Bonner Snr

Above: *With the quaint fire station, stone cottages and distant fells, the scene can only be Cumbria, the North West's most picturesque county. A 1982 Dodge G75C/Carmichael water ladder (TRM 781X) basks in the sunshine at Lazonby in the Vale of Eden.* Tony Kent

Left: *An equally unmistakeable North West location - Blackpool. Although the former borough brigade had operated a Bedford TK/Merryweather turntable ladder of its own, similar to that depicted, VTB 321D is actually one of four purchased by Lancashire County Fire Brigade in the 1960s. Originally serving in the textile town of Nelson, it looks slightly uncomfortable parked among the illuminations, tramcar and tower at the famous North West resort.* Tony Kent

Birkenhead, Chester & Wallasey (1948-1974)

Above: *The* Thunderbird*; this rare AEC/Merryweather of Birkenhead Fire Brigade was a favourite of both enthusiasts and local fire fighters alike. The appliance was so well known on Merseyside that, when driving it away from Birkenhead in 1967 for a life in preservation, the new owner was stopped at the Mersey Tunnel by a keen traffic policeman who thought the vehicle must have been stolen! Although delivered with a wheeled escape,* Thunderbird *is photographed in its later guise as a pump-ladder, by which time the original AEC radiator and grill had also been replaced by this rather utilitarian version.*

The County of Cheshire had just four borough brigades, and all but one of these were situated at the western end of the county, with the conjoined Birkenhead and Wallasey occupying one corner of the Wirral peninsular opposite Liverpool. Both towns chose to operate joint fire and ambulance services, and each had an extensive dock network which brought them into frequent contact with each other and occasionally, through their separate Mersey Tunnel road links with Liverpool as well. Wallasey was also responsible for the seaside resort of New Brighton.

The City of Chester meanwhile, was the only borough brigade in the region to have a boundary with a different country (Wales)! Indeed, many of its calls were over the border, as well as into Cheshire. Birkenhead was the earliest to be motorised with the purchase of one of the first Dennis appliances in 1909. The majority of pre-war machines would however be Leyland, including an 85ft Metz wooden turntable of 1928. Ten years later, Chester acquired a seven-year-old Dennis/Morris-Magirus ladder from the London Fire Brigade.

With a working height of only 85ft, this appliance could fit into Chester's picturesque, but cramped, "black and white" fire station in Northgate Street. By the time the NFS began to supply new turntables in the 1940s, the shortcomings of the 1931 Dennis were apparent, and a new Dennis/ Merryweather (still equipped with just an 85ft ladder) was issued after a few years' service in North Wales. Wallasey, meanwhile, which had never previously operated a TL, was supplied with one of the few Austin K4 60ft Merryweathers to be posted to the region.

Top Left: Thunderbird'*s stable-mate at the Whetstone Lane fire station was the equally unusual* W.E.R. Short*, a Dennis F2 model of 1953. The Rolls Royce-engined, normal-control F2 was more commonly fitted with open bodywork and the enclosed body fitted to the Birkenhead appliance clearly owes much to the more familiar products from the Guildford factory such as the F7. The later embellishments such as blue beacon and trafficators take nothing away from the racy appearance of this vehicle.* Joe Hain

Centre Left: *The post-war Wallasey fleet included no less than six different Dennis models, from the diminutive F8 up to the larger F44. This F43 pump escape from 1971 (JHF 707J) was the last pumping appliance purchased by the brigade and is seen in the characteristic yellow livery at the Mill Lane headquarters.* Jack Robertson Collection - FBS North West

Bottom Left: *Chester's attractive Wilsdon-bodied Bedford S-Type of 1958 (34 GFM) stands outside the city's picturesque fire station in Northgate Street, which dated from 1911. The appliance was originally conceived as a multi-purpose machine, with foam and salvage equipment carried, but was soon operating as a normal "major pump." The lack of space in the black-and-white building meant that the adjoining Northgate Brewery yard was sometimes used for drill purposes.* Joe Hain

The first post-war appliances to be purchased by Birkenhead were highly unusual. One (a Merryweather limousine pump escape delivered in 1952), was built on a much-modified AEC Regent III chassis, a type that had been launched for PSV application three years earlier. Despite good export sales, most British fire chiefs disliked the normal control layout so it fell to Birkenhead to purchase the only UK example. In accordance with BFB tradition, it was christened *T. H. Herron*, but soon earned the nickname Thunderbird, thanks to its powerful appearance and roaring Meadows petrol engine.

Soon afterwards this appliance was joined by another interesting limousine, this time one based on a Dennis F2 chassis. Again, this was a model more common to overseas customers or industrial brigades. A rear-mounted pump, suited to the dockside risks, was specified for both vehicles and together these two machines added a wonderful touch of character to the streets of Birkenhead.

Deliveries over the next few years were mainly HCB-bodied Bedford chassis, along with an unusual Commer foam tender supplied by Sun Engineering and a 1960 AEC/Merryweather turntable, fitted with the ladders from a 20-year old Leyland. The AEC/Merryweather combination was also chosen for new-build turntables at both Wallasey and Chester in the same period, the latter being something of a "squeeze" in the Northgate Street station.

Such limitations of space would remain a problem for the brigade until new premises were opened in 1971, and may have played a part in the selection of a neat, short-wheelbase Bedford S-Type appliance received in 1958. This was one of only a couple of pumps in the region to be bodied by Wilsdon of Solihull and looked very attractive with its streamlined bodywork and black-painted mudguards.

On the disbandment of the Auxiliary Fire Service in 1968, several brigades purchased surplus vehicles, notably the Bedford S- and RL-types (better known as the Green Goddess pumps), as the Home Office reduced the number of emergency appliances. Chester took this opportunity to boost its special appliance fleet with one Plaxton-bodied "Goddess" – which it converted to a foam tender – and a Land Rover Series II soft-top, fitted out as a road accident unit. About this time there was some experimentation nationally with fire engine colour schemes, particularly with the famous "Coventry Yellow." The only brigade to opt for this scheme in the North West region was Wallasey, which re-painted the unusual Commer Walk-Thru emergency tender and three Dennis pumps in yellow. The Dennis' still bore this livery when the brigade was amalgamated into the new Merseyside Fire Brigade in 1974.

Below: *Shoppers in Chester's historic two-tier "Rows" stop to watch a "working job" in Bridge Street in February 1973. In attendance at the fire in the Owen Owen's department store, are a 1962 Dennis F28 pump (1818 FM) and a 1972 Dennis F108 water tender (UFM 379K), the last new appliance to be delivered to the brigade prior to the 1974 local government reorganisation. The Perkins-engined Dennis F108 was chosen by several of the county borough brigades in this region and embodied the traditional features and build quality which suited customers who bought appliances one at a time. A five-speed manual gearbox and the well-proven Dennis No.2 600-gpm pump were standard. The hinged lockers and wooden extension ladders, seen on both Chester appliances, are also characteristic "borough" specifications.* Cheshire Observer Series

Above: *The Warrington brigade was prominent in the development of foam-producing appliances. For example, this 1958 Bedford S-Type foam tender (SED 999), with locally-made Marsden bodywork, was adapted to become one of the first high-expansion foam units in the country.*

St. Helens, Warrington & Wigan (1948-1974)

That part of Lancashire stretching between Liverpool and Manchester, north of the River Mersey, was quite different from the Pennine regions to the east of the county. The area included the South Lancashire coalfield, and for many years was characterised by pits and assorted heavy industries such as railways, chemicals and glass. There were some cotton mills in and around Wigan itself but these represented only the fringe of Lancashire's textile belt. When the local government boundaries were re-drawn in 1974, the three boroughs discussed in this chapter were each transferred into completely separate counties (Merseyside, Cheshire and Greater Manchester).

Wigan most closely resembled a traditional Lancashire borough brigade, having been police-controlled until World War II. On the post-war handover from the NFS the brigade inherited, along with the usual austerity appliances, a 1935 Merryweather turntable ladder originally from Hornsey in Middlesex.

A Whitson-bodied Commer water tender and a Dennis F12 were the first new purchases, whilst the 1952 conversion of a wartime Fordson water tender by coachbuilders Cuerden provided the brigade with a stopgap emergency tender until a new Bedford with HCB body was purchased ten years later.

Two pumps by the same builders and a further Dennis made up the establishment. All but the most recent carried names, with a "999" registration system being utilised for part of the fleet. The earliest fire engine to bear such a mark was probably a Belsize/John Morris pump escape commissioned by St. Helens in 1911 (DJ 999). However, as this plate pre-dated the introduction of the emergency telephone number by several years, it is merely coincidental.

Apart from a 1952 Commer with Carmichael coachwork, for 20 years the St. Helens fleet was mainly made up of various Dennis machines; including an F24 of 1957 fitted with the earlier style of radiator grill. Until 1959, the appliances were housed in a totally inadequate fire station in Parade Street. This was located at the rear of the Town Hall, from which appliances emerged, French-style, through a single doorway. The first delivery to the new Headquarters on Parr Stocks Road was an AEC/Merryweather hydraulic turntable, bought new in 1960 to replace a 60ft wartime Austin.

In 1967 the brigade turned to the Leyland group, beginning with a Carmichael-built Albion emergency tender, which would later receive a distinctive white livery. Next came a 1969 Leyland Beaver fitted with Carmichael's Swedish-designed "Orbitor" platform and three Leyland pumps, all with the same "Ergomatic" cab, but finished by different bodybuilders and painted from the outset in a striking white and red livery.

No less distinctive were the unusual appliances operated by Warrington Fire Services, as the brigade was called at this time. Under its young chief officer, Harry Beckingham, it was to become recognised as one of the most innovative fire authorities in the country. Surrounded by several major chemical risk premises, it pioneered the use of high-expansion foam equipment, and in the mid-1960s converted an existing Bedford foam tender into the country's first Hi-Expansion Foam Unit.

In 1964 the brigade unveiled its first "multi-purpose appliance; outwardly a normal water tender, the vehicle (built by Busmar of Blackpool on a 6-ton Bedford TK chassis) combined the functions of pump, emergency tender, salvage tender and foam tender, the latter function being achieved with a separate foam pump and 45-gallon tank. It was claimed that its four-man crew could undertake tasks previously needing up to twelve!

Over the next four years, two further Bedford TK "multis" were completed by HCB-Angus, developing the theme by adding even more equipment such as a wheeled escape, high-expansion foam generator and compressed air system, which could simultaneously recharge breathing apparatus and supply pneumatic-power tools.

I had hoped to illustrate one of these appliances, NED 101G, but was defeated by a lack of space. Delivered in 1968, it represented the third and final stage in the development of these unique vehicles. The HCB-Angus bodied Bedford was described as a "complete fire-fighting and rescue unit," with a 200-gallon water tank, power tools, lighting, breathing apparatus, 5000 cu ft/min air compressor and a high-expansion foam generator which could operate either in portable mode or directly from the appliance through the rear locker.

Top Right: *Originally delivered in the traditional red, but seen wearing its later white-and-red livery, is St. Helens' 1967 Albion Chieftain emergency tender with Carmichael bodywork (LDJ 999E). The word "Rescue" was added at the same time as the repaint, to reflect the service's wider role. The appliance subsequently became part of the Merseyside Fire Brigade fleet.* Jack Robertson collection – FBS North West

Centre Right: *The familiar, stylish profile of the Whitson bodywork is clearly shown in a view of this Commer water tender delivered to Wigan in 1950. Named* Lewis, *it was one of only two appliances by this builder to operate in the region's county borough brigades, the other example going to Bolton.*

Bottom Right: *This Dennis-Metz 100ft turntable ladder (CJP 800) was acquired by Wigan Fire Brigade in 1957 and christened* Somers. *It was taken out of service in 1976 after collapsing during a drill session on the station yard.* Joe Hain

Blackburn, Bolton & Burnley (1948-1974)

The county boroughs of Blackburn, Bolton and Burnley, nestling among the West Pennine moors could be said to represent the archetypal Lancashire textile towns, having spawned such famous sons as Samuel Crompton and James Hargreaves. Whilst Bolton was known for its "fine" cotton spinning, the other two were most definitely centres of weaving – an important distinction in Lancashire.

In fire brigade terms, the vehicle fleets of the three mill towns each followed their own distinctive trends, with no similarities so far as front-line appliances were concerned, though there existed a certain amount of commonality with the special appliances. Burnley and Blackburn had both chosen Merryweather for their earliest motor fire pumps, but the latter was also well known for a 3-axle Thornycroft acquired in 1931. Bolton had been a staunch Leyland customer since buying its first one in 1913.

Yet, apart from one single Commer water tender, Bolton's post-war pumps were all AEC/Merryweather, beginning with a classic Regent pump escape bought in 1951; five Marquis pumps came later on. Consequently the town's fleet of handsome AEC/Merryweather appliances made a welcome change from the numerous Bedford and Dennis machines found elsewhere in the region. In 1951 a local coachbuilder, Bellhouse, Hartwell & Co. Ltd. of Westhoughton, constructed the bodywork for an interesting new appliance on Commer chassis. This vehicle (EBN 706) was one of the few "proper" salvage tenders to be operated in the North West, as most brigades combined this role with that of an emergency tender. Laden with canvas sheets, mops, buckets and other equipment, the salvage tender would assist crews at mill fires, and other incidents, in protecting property from water damage and so on.

The following year Bellhouse, Hartwell carried out an extensive rebuild of a 1939 Bedford heavy pump unit (FYH 85) converting it to a useful emergency tender. This vehicle lasted until 1966 when a new Bedford TK emergency tender was purchased, with Dennis "M" series bodywork. The range had been so named when Dennis acquired the former Alfred Miles company in 1962 and began to supply bodywork on any make of chassis. The earlier Bedford had been part of a large batch of wartime pumps and its sister appliance (FYH 83) could be found at Blackburn. Coincidentally, this vehicle also received a very similar new emergency tender body at the hands of the brigade's own tradesmen in 1950.

Top Left: *This smart salvage tender belonging to Bolton Fire Brigade (EBN 706) was built in 1951 by Bellhouse, Hartwell & Co. Ltd. on a modified Commer chassis*

Centre Left: *In the whole of the North West only Bolton operated examples of the famous AEC/Merryweather Marquis model. Its first, NWH 600 of 1959, is seen at the town's Moor Lane fire station.* Bob Bonner Snr.

Bottom Left: *Blackburn's first post-war machine was this Bedford SB 600gpm pump (ECB 440), with streamlined Wilsdon coachwork, delivered in January 1954. It was named* John Charnley *after the Chairman of the Watch and Fire Services Committee.*

The Blackburn fleet showed some interesting differences from its neighbours. The first new appliance was a 1954 Bedford SB pump, on the shortened passenger coach chassis, with streamlined coachwork by Wilsdon, a combination seen in great numbers in Birmingham. Named *John Charnley* in honour of the Chairman, this appliance set the pattern for further "namers" in the fleet. Among other unusual vehicles in Blackburn were the 1957 Dennis F15 pump escape (HCB 500), with a rear-mounted pump (which is now preserved and also features as a Corgi model) and a 1967 emergency tender, based on the 3-ton Bedford J-type van.

The latter was fitted with normal Hawson bodywork, but extensively fitted-out internally by station personnel. A smaller Bedford appliance, on a long-wheelbase CALZ chassis/cab, was fitted out as a chimney tender, these fires once being an everyday occurrence in the town's many terraced properties. Interestingly, none of the special appliances, including the turntable ladder, were considered worthy of being given a name.

It would be 1955 before Burnley acquired any new stock, when they obtained a standard Dennis F12 pump escape. At this time the brigade was still running a 1932 Leyland-Metz turntable with an 85ft wooden ladder, originally belonging to Blackpool. This was finally retired in 1958 on the arrival of an attractive new Merryweather on an AEC Mercury chassis, one of 14 examples of this popular combination to reach the North West. Bolton and Blackburn both replaced wartime vehicles with the same type eight years later.

All three of these most traditional of Lancashire brigades operated some Leylands before the war but, apart from the short-lived Firemaster project in 1959-63, the company had not built any more fire engines. There was therefore great interest in 1963 when Burnley took delivery of a prototype water tender by John Morris & Sons Ltd. The vehicle, on a 125bhp Leyland chassis, also marked Morris's return to the field of full-size fire engines, although the actual bodywork was contracted out to another company, Kerbell Bodies of Stockport.

In 1964 the Brigade went one step further with the purchase of another Leyland/Morris, but fitted with a 50ft Simon Snorkel platform. At this period, the fire service in general was still evaluating the role of the Snorkel, and Burnley's unique machine experimentally combined the functions of aerial appliance and emergency tender. Bolton Fire Brigade purchased a more "normal" hydraulic platform, an 85ft ERF/Simon, in 1971.

Interestingly, Burnley, Bolton and Blackburn all chose the identical appliance for their last ever purchases. Within months of each other in 1972, all three commissioned a Perkins-engined Dennis F108, Blackburn's, of course, being named – *John Beardsworth*.

Top Right: *Blackburn's 1968 emergency tender (HCB 999F) was based on the standard, Hawson-bodied 3-ton Bedford J-Type, extensively fitted-out in-house to carry eight breathing apparatus, a generator and a full range of rescue equipment*

Bottom Right: *In 1964, Burnley commissioned this combined 50ft Simon Snorkel hydraulic platform/emergency tender on a Leyland chassis. Supplied by John Morris, it was the Salford firm's last aerial appliance.* John Morris official works photograph, D.W.Plant collection.

MANCHESTER, SALFORD & STOCKPORT (1948-1974)

The closest-knit of all the North West's borough brigades, the authorities for Manchester, Salford and Stockport occupied a 62-square mile conurbation at the junction of Lancashire and Cheshire. Whilst Stockport and Salford brigades both shared borders with their big city brother, Salford had the closer relationship, through a long history of joint attendance at fires. In the 19th century there was considerable rivalry between the two and in a famous incident in 1846, the respective chief officers came only just short of fisticuffs on the fireground!

Manchester actually had the distinction of forming England's first properly-funded municipal fire service in 1826, and they were at the forefront of many innovations.

The city's earliest motor appliance, a Dennis, came in 1911 followed by several from the local manufacturers Belsize-John Morris. Some unusual Ford TT and Bedford WS appliances were bodied in-house, a practice continued after the war with the re-building of ex-NFS vehicles. As recounted earlier, the war years were a turbulent time for Manchester and substantial re-building was required in the years that followed.

The 1950s fleet was characterised by a number of innovative appliances, beginning with a highly unusual Dennis F18 of 1954. With an experimental General Motors "Hydra-matic" gearbox, it was the first commercial vehicle in Britain to have automatic transmission. A second F18 with broadly similar specification followed in 1956, leading to the development by Dennis, of its popular automatic F24 range the following year.

Left: *In a truly action-packed picture, we see one of the best-known appliances in Manchester. This was a 1954 Dennis F18 (NXJ 45), the first UK fire engine with automatic transmission. The huge chrome bumpers protect the 500-gpm Carl Metz dual-pressure fire pump, mounted in front of the engine, whilst the limousine body with sliding doors was produced by Bankfield of Southport. Though delivered with a wheeled escape, this was later removed and NXJ 45 spent most of its life at Great Jackson Street fire station, from where it responded to this fire in Hulme in 1966.*

Top Right: *The Manchester fleet was synonymous with the Leyland Firemaster, launched in 1959. A front-mounted pump and high-pressure hose reels were features of the three pump escape versions whilst the emergency tender supplied in 1962 had a winch in place of the pump. Standing by at a small supermarket fire in Longsight in 1967 is 7596 N, built by Cocker in 1960 and the second of two similar appliances to be stationed at the city's main fire station in London Road. Clearly visible is the single nearside door, through which all the crew (other than the driver) had to enter and alight, negotiating several steps in the process. This arrangement was due to the high floor level, caused by the forward pump position. Unusually the engine cover panel is missing in this view of the appliance.*

Centre Right: *The brigade turned to Albions (another division of the Leyland group) for the chassis for its next 14 pumps. Despite a heavy, manual gear-change, the six-speed Albions were surprisingly sprightly and deceptively manoeuvrable. Three separate builders produced the same "MFB look", with wrap-around windscreens. The first Carmichael-bodied example (ONF 664H) is seen soon after entering service at Upton Street in 1970.*

Bottom Right: *This 1939 Leyland pump of Salford Fire Brigade, formerly with open bodywork, was completely re-bodied in 1953 and remained on the fleet for a further ten years. The design appears to have been influenced by the brigade's recent Dennis deliveries. Salford was one of the earliest users in the area of the 45ft alloy extension ladder.* Vince Gillibrand

The year 1959 saw the debut of the Leyland Firemaster, developed jointly with Leyland Motors. Described as a "new conception" in fire engine design, the Firemaster pump escape featured a 150bhp Leyland under-floor engine, semi-automatic transmission and Sigmund 900-gpm pump mounted at the front behind folding doors. It was considered a huge success in Manchester but attempts to influence the wider market were less so, only six other versions joining Manchester's three pump escapes and one emergency tender.

After the last Firemaster arrived in 1963, the MFB stayed loyal to the Leyland group, receiving the first of many Albion pumps in 1966. The next seven years saw successive deliveries of the Fire Chief model, bodied variously by Cocker, HCB-Angus and Carmichael. A foam tender and two salvage tenders were also Albion-based, whilst a Leyland power unit was chosen for the brigade's 1964 Bedford TK/Simon hydraulic platform.

Top Left: *Proudly bearing the operating authority's name in large lettering below its cab window, this unique 65ft Simon Snorkel (MBA 773F), was intended to replace a pump escape in Salford. It was specified with a double cab, 500-gpm pump, 270-gal water tank, breathing apparatus and an extension ladder mounted on the nearside of the body. The styling of this appliance, even though it is over 35-years old at the time of publication, still has a modern feel to it - compared to some offerings of the 1960s, one could even call it futuristic.* Fred Barnes

Centre Left: *Resembling the new John Morris pumps of the same year, this 1965 Commer water tender of Stockport Fire Brigade (EDB 999C) was built by Kerbell Bodies in the town; thus reflecting Stockport's policy to 'buy locally made products where and when ever possible.' The pump and various other parts had been salvaged from a 1956 Dennis F24, written-off in a serious accident. Unfortunately, this product from the Rootes Group (produced like Bedford in Dunstable) was somewhat underpowered for Stockport's steep hills, and as a consequence it soon earned the unflattering nickname "Puffing Billy."*

Bottom Left: *Also bodied by Kerbell, was another Cheshire-built ERF, this time an 84PF water tender for Stockport (UDB 675J). One of two long-wheelbase (12ft 6in) versions for that brigade, it was delivered in 1971, and is seen here at an incident in Lavender Brow the following year.* Bob Bonner Snr

Across the River Irwell, the City of Salford Fire Department (as it was known) had a slightly more traditional fleet, but one that nevertheless included some interesting examples. In 1948 the city's main fire station was still home to a number of pre-war Leylands, but all future pumps would be of Dennis make. One F12 model in 1954 was one of the earliest to carry a 45ft alloy ladder and had non-standard rear-end styling to suit.

The brigade's own firemen-mechanics were responsible for a complete rebuild of one of the Leylands, also the bodying of a Bedford TK foam tender in 1966. The most interesting Salford vehicle of the period was a 1968 ERF/HCB-Angus/Simon Snorkel, designed to function as a fully-crewed front-line machine, complete with tank, pump and a full range of equipment. The idea soon proved unworkable, as the 36ft long machine was far too clumsy for Salford's terraced streets, and it was downgraded to a two-man special appliance.

Manchester's other neighbour, Stockport, had also opted for Dennis after the war, sharing (with Warrington) one of the only two "high-coachline" F15 water tenders to serve in the region. After replacing its wartime Dennis-Merryweather turntable ladder in 1963 with a particularly good-looking AEC Mercury/Haydon-Magirus version, the hatting-town turned to Commer, for two interesting appliances in the 1960s.

One, a 1967 emergency salvage tender by Kerbell, was only the first such appliance in the brigade. It attended its first major incident in June of that year when a DC4 airliner crashed near the town centre. The last years of Stockport Fire Brigade saw the build-up of a fine fleet of ERF appliances, some by Kerbell, others by Jennings, and including a Simon 50ft pump hydraulic platform.

Liverpool Salvage Corps (1842-1984)

In September 1842 Liverpool suffered a devastating fire that destroyed nearly seven acres of valuable warehousing, consequently the insurance firms soon afterwards set up a unique organisation to remove property and take care of salvage. Thus was born the Liverpool Salvage Corps, later officially titled The Fire Salvage Association of Liverpool Limited. Similar bodies were founded in London (1866) and Glasgow (1873).

Liverpool was the first to become motorised when, in 1911, two Dennis motor salvage tenders were commissioned. The solid-tyred machines had similar "Braidwood" style bodywork to normal fire engines, but without ladders or pump; the bodies of both were transferred to new Chevrolet chassis around 1930. A second-hand ex-WD Canadian Military Pattern Chevrolet chassis was then acquired in 1946 and bodied by a local firm, Pearson Brothers. In the early 1950s the Corps purchased two Austin K8 tenders and by 1956 they had a pair of Commers, with locally-built Sandon bodywork. Other small firms, including Davidson, Charterway and Harwin, supplied the bodywork for later vehicles, mainly on Ford and Mercedes-Benz chassis. To better describe the function of the fleet, the term "salvage tender" was dropped in favour of "damage control unit."

The Corps had a special relationship with the Liverpool Fire Brigade, its station at Derby Road being linked to the LFB control room in order to receive and monitor fire calls. All the Corps' appliances carried a red livery, with the same warning devices and road traffic privileges as ordinary fire engines. Its personnel wore similar uniforms to the local brigade and operated a round-the-clock, disciplined service. As well as its front-line fleet, the Corps operated various ancillary vehicles, including lorries, vans and mobile cranes, the last of these being an Iron Fairy of 1970. Sadly, in 1984, the insurance industry disbanded all three UK fire salvage corps, leaving this type of operation to the regular fire service. A new Merseyside Salvage Corps, formed later that year by ex-employees, proved to be short-lived.

Top Right: *One of two Chevrolet tenders built in 1929/30 utilising the bodywork from the 1911 Dennis motor salvage wagons. These vehicles, having the advantage of an enclosed cab, lasted until the 1940s, one being destroyed in the Liverpool Blitz.*

Centre Right: *Another rebuild, this ex-Canadian military pattern Chevrolet was recycled by Liverpool motor engineers Pearson's in 1946, in a style also seen on some of their other products. The illuminated "Salvage Corps" sign also appeared on other members of the fleet and may have had its origins in the wartime blackout.* Trans-Pennine Archive

Bottom Right: *This Commer salvage tender (UKD 987) was a familiar sight around Liverpool for many years. It was built by a local firm called Sandon, who also supplied two smaller appliances on Ford Thames chassis. To the left can be seen one of the Davidson-bodied Ford D-series tenders and, in the rear yard, the Thames Trader lorry which was used to bring fire- and water-damaged cotton bales back to the Corps' warehouse for re-processing.*

Above: *Several Cheshire stations operated Land Rover pumps, initially all being normal control models, but in 1962 the county acquired its first forward control model, (557 WTU) for Stockton Heath station. A Carmichael Redwing FT/6, it was based on a converted 109-in. long wheelbase chassis, fitted with a 100-gallon water tank and a 20-gpm hose reel pump.* Carmichael

CHESHIRE (1948-1974)

The fourth of the region's county brigades was Cheshire, whose Headquarters at Dee Banks were actually within the City of Chester. More than three quarters of the brigade area was classed as rural, but there were some significant industrial pockets too. These included Ellesmere Port, which contained refineries and chemicals, the silk town of Macclesfield and the cotton mills around Hyde and Stalybridge to the north-east. The new brigade inherited the usual mixture of pre-war appliances, mainly Dennis and Leyland, but a number of wartime heavy units and some Bedford QL water carriers were also bequeathed by the outgoing National Fire Service.

The first new machine to be registered was a Dennis F7 pump escape in 1950, followed by some Commer water tenders by various bodybuilders, including old-established Cheshire firm, J H Jennings of Sandbach. Among the more interesting vehicles at this time were two Windover-bodied Leyland Comet water tenders, of normal control layout.

Even more unusual were the six Thornycroft Nubian water tenders purchased by Cheshire between 1951 and 1953. A model more familiar in the role of airfield crash tender, these four-wheel-drive mammoths were located at stations in and around the Delamere Forest, such as Northwich. Carmichael bodywork was fitted, with 500-gallon water tanks.

Yet, apart from the exceptions described, virtually the whole of Cheshire's pumps were Dennis. Over 70 were ordered between 1950 and 1972, giving the brigade one of the largest such fleets. Several of these comprised the diminutive F8 model, specially designed for rural areas, with a 7ft wheelbase and 6ft 6in overall width.

Other types of Dennis were also utilised, although these were generally the narrower (7ft) models such as the F24 and F38, which Cheshire had finished with unpainted alloy bodywork. In tandem with this fleet of tidy, well-kept Dennis water tenders, most stations also operated a Land Rover L4P (*light four-wheel-drive pump*). The earliest examples were to quite a basic design, utilising the standard long-wheelbase pick-up; later on a number of these were converted for use as high-expansion foam tenders. In 1962, however, the brigade took delivery of its first Carmichael Redwing FT6 foam tender, with forward control enclosed bodywork.

Over the next eight years several more were purchased with one particular example (AMB 587B at Sandbach), being immortalised in the well-known Matchbox model. Modernisation of the brigade's special appliance fleet, which consisted mainly of converted ex-NFS stock, also began in the 1960s. Four new emergency tenders on Bedford TK chassis were commissioned using three bodybuilders, and on delivery they were sent to all corners of the county. Two of these, at Knutsford and Crewe, would give many years of service protecting Cheshire's section of the M6 motorway.

The wartime turntable ladders at Hyde and Crewe were disposed of and a new 70ft ERF/Simon Snorkel platform was bought in 1969 for Ellesmere Port. Macclesfield's 1938 Leyland-Metz turntable ladder was replaced in 1967 by a Merryweather 100ft ladder on a Bedford TK. Probably the most interesting special appliance of Cheshire Fire Brigade during this pre-1974 period was NKF 470F, Ellesmere Port's four-axle ERF 68GX bulk foam tanker. It was formerly owned by Yates' haulage company and was converted by the brigade to carry 3,000 gallons of foam compound.

Obviously satisfied with its two ERF special appliances, the brigade turned again to the Sandbach company in 1972 when the first of a small batch of Jennings-built pumps joined the existing one-make fleet. However, this all-Cheshire product would never reach the same numbers as Dennis in the county.

Top Right: *Looking for all the world like something you would find on an airfield, this 1951 Thornycroft Nubian 4x4 water tender with Carmichael body (NTU 606) turns out of the old Frodsham fire station, Cheshire, in 1970.* Charles Jones

Centre Right: *The Cheshire Fire Brigade soon settled on Dennis for normal pumping appliances and remained a very good customer of the Guildford-based company for around 20 years. In action at the sort of rural fire scene familiar to the county's fire-fighters is TTU 63D, from Sale station, a characteristically neat Dennis F38 model of 1966. The bumper-mounted electric bell clearly seen here was standard specification in this brigade.*

Bottom Right: *Cheshire's first ERF water ladder (FLG 647K), powered by a Rolls Royce engine drives through Sandbach. This was the home of its renowned chassis builder, whilst the coachwork was also built locally by J H Jennings. The glass-fibre cab with panoramic windscreen certainly enhanced the looks of what was already a technically superior North West product. It was posted to Northwich in 1972.* ERF Ltd.

CUMBRIA (1974 TO DATE)

The local government reorganisation of 1st April 1974 resulted in sweeping changes to local fire services. Overnight, the fascinating North West mix of four county council and twenty-two county borough brigades was replaced with just five county authorities. The two "metropolitan" conurbations of Merseyside and Greater Manchester, along with Cumbria, formed brand new brigades, whilst Lancashire and Cheshire effectively continued as they were, but with territorial changes.

With an area of 2,680 square miles, Cumbria Fire Service was geographically the largest in the region and at the same time, the quietest in operational terms, apart from the larger stations such as Carlisle and Barrow-in-Furness. As well as these two constituents, the new brigade saw the amalgamation of Cumberland and Westmorland also gained the whole of the Furness district from Lancashire and the Sedbergh station from the West Riding of Yorkshire. The latter came in with an unusual all-terrain appliance, a former demonstrator dating from 1968 based on the Steyr Puch Haflinger from Austria. This was in fact another North West product, having been built at Goodwood Motor Bodies in Rochdale and marketed by Schofield of Bury.

Above: *Stationed at Bootle (the rural one) was CHH 243T, a 1979 Ford A0609 with Attack bodywork by G & T of Gravesend, Kent. It was Cumbria's first type of 'small' fire appliance using the snub-nosed, 3-litre A-series (or "overgrown Transit") chassis.* Tony Kent

The rest of the fleet comprised of various Bedford, Ford and Land Rover machines, with some Commers and Karriers still in service. The first new appliances consisted of Carmichael and ERF-bodied water tenders on the Ford D1114 chassis. One of the Ford / Carmichael acquisitions (NHH 176P formerly at Coniston and Broughton) has been preserved by the editor of this book.

An even smaller Ford made its debut during 1976, in the shape of the Attack lightweight appliance, specially developed for Cumbria by G & T Fire Control Ltd. This experimental unit was designed to cope with both hilly and narrow roads. It carried a full crew, with all the normal equipment and ladders, but under 200 gallons of water. Four of the new Fords were followed in 1980 by a slightly larger, Dodge-based G & T machine, named the Advance. The big problem was finding the right size of vehicle to suit Cumbria's difficult operating environment, to say nothing of the many older, restricted fire stations still in service.

Top Right: *After the Attack range, the brigade tried this Dodge G75 with Advance body, also by G & T (GHH 923V). It carried a 13.5-metre alloy extension ladder and was based at Ambleside, in the Lake District National Park.* Tony Kent

Centre Right: *A small fleet of rescue units with locally-built bodywork was commissioned in the mid-1980s including D426 TAO, a Dodge G12 by Kendal Coachworks, seen at the fire station in that town.* Tony Kent

Bottom Right: *The Cumbria "compact" water tender is exemplified by L217 KAO, a Leyland DAF T45-160 built by HCB-Angus to the brigade's design, seen at Millom.* Tony Kent

Several more Dodge appliances were commissioned between 1979 and 1987, beginning with thirteen water tenders on the G12 chassis, bodied by Anglo Coachbuilders. Subsequent Dodge deliveries on both G75 and G13 series had Carmichael bodywork. The brigade's special appliances were, for a long time, also mainly from the Chrysler/Renault stable. A small fleet of Westmorland-style rescue tenders, using the Walk-Thru van, had been delivered in the late-1970s, but were later displaced by the short-wheelbase G12 "rescue units" from local firms like Kendal Coachworks and Edmund Crow. The Haydon-Magirus turntable ladders at Carlisle and Barrow were transferred to new 16-ton Dodge chassis around 1981, while yet more Dodges were bodied as "special incident units" in 1987.

A sizeable fleet of Volvo water tenders has been operated since 1988, these were bodied firstly by Carmichael and, more recently the Scottish firm, Emergency One. Three new Carmichael-Magirus turntable ladders, on Volvo FL6.16 chassis, were also delivered in 1988-1990 for Carlisle, Barrow and Workington. The need for a smaller vehicle was still recognised and in 1991 the brigade re-appraised its requirements for rural appliances, with particular emphasis on stowage space and overall vehicle size.

All fire authorities were carrying more equipment, especially bulky rescue equipment for road traffic accidents, but Cumbria's roads and farm gateways were not getting any wider. The brigade therefore set itself the seemingly impossible task of making the appliance smaller and the locker space larger! Without the retrograde step of reducing the water capacity, the solution lay in a radical alteration to the positioning of both the tank and the pump unit. By designing a "T-shaped" plastic tank, set low between the chassis rails, the new layout achieved a lighter overall weight, lower centre of gravity and additional locker space at a stroke. Not surprisingly, the appliance was called the "compact" water tender; the prototype, by Carmichael on a Leyland DAF 45-160 chassis, was exhibited at the *Fire 91 Exhibition* prior to entering service at Coniston.

Twelve were supplied between 1991 and 1994, some based on Volvo and using two different bodybuilders, but the brigade has since returned to full-size water tenders for the time being. The latest Cumbria concept appliance is the "multi-purpose vehicle" which, as its name implies, fulfils several functions at the same time, including foam tender and environmental protection unit. Based on a Volvo FL6 chassis, the MPV built by Emergency One also carries a Kawasaki Mule all-terrain vehicle, especially chosen to traverse some of the higher or more difficult parts of the Cumbria area.

Lancashire (1974 To Date)

Above: *The prototype Leyland Freighter/Fulton & Wylie pump (D100 TRN) undergoing performance testing at the Leyland Vehicles Technical Centre in June 1986. Note the unfinished GRP crew cab and the brake-testing equipment affixed to the front bumper.* Lancashire Fire & Rescue Service

The 1974 reorganisation saw Lancashire lose stations to the new Merseyside, Greater Manchester and Cumbria authorities, yet simultaneously absorb the former borough brigades of Blackpool, Preston, Blackburn and Burnley along with two former West Riding of Yorkshire stations, namely those at Barnoldswick and Earby.

The LCFB fleet was thus joined by some unfamiliar AEC, Leyland and Dennis appliances, including one of the famous white-painted Dennis F46 models from the West Riding; no time was wasted in applying a lick of red paint to remind this interloper that it was now serving the "red rose" county! The first new deliveries during 1975-76, were 14 ERFs, fitted with the firm's own Firefighter coachwork. The same bodybuilder and its successor (Cheshire Fire Engineering) was selected for the next wave of appliances, on Ford D1114, Ford D1617 and Bedford TK chassis. The Bedfords, delivered from 1980, incorporated a number of special features and were termed "new generation" appliances by the brigade.

Based on the latest CFE design with full-width, steel-framed safety cab, the new appliances had Allison automatic gearboxes, easy-access and crew seat belts. The most noticeable change however was the water capacity, virtually halved from the normal 1,800-litres (400-galls) to just 1,000-litres (220-galls), saving almost a ton with consequent improvements to stability and braking.

To accompany the new pumps, the brigade also launched its "new generation" special appliances, based on the Powell Duffryn "Rolonof" demountable body system. These included a chemical incident unit, foam carrier, breathing apparatus tender and two ancillary "pods" to be transported by a pair of Ford D1314 prime movers based at Preston. Unfortunately lack of space prevents our illustrating this system.

Top Right: *A 1975 ERF "Firefighter" water ladder (LHG 317N), photographed at Nelson, showing a clear contrast between the part-fluorescent/part glossy red paint finish used by the Lancashire brigade.* Alastair Collins

Centre Right: *Here is one of the "new generation" Bedford TK/CFE pumps with the 220-gallon tanks, this one (VFV 728V) entered service at Burnley in 1980; sadly before the decade was out the great Bedford name was no more, and having been abandoned by General Motors, it left the way for other manufacturers to take over.* Tony Kent collection

Bottom Right: *The "Tupperware" fire engine: One of Lancashire's latest Leyland DAF 55/TVAC/Plastisol pumps at Fulwood (Y543 XEO), showing the striking new livery now employed.*

The lightweight Bedfords served their purpose, but by 1984 Lancashire had its sights on another new model that (with significant technical input by the brigade) would once again make an old-established manufacturer the centre of fire service interest. That year, Leyland had launched its new truck chassis, which soon caught the eye of the brigade's innovative Transport Officer, John Taylor and the result of this is illustrated in the picture on the facing page.

It is an interesting story, for close liaison between the brigade and Leyland Vehicles Ltd resulted in substantial modifications to the standard T45 Freighter (including modifications to the frame height, transmission, suspension and braking), to produce an impressive new fire engine chassis, complying with strict Home Office performance standards. Fulton & Wylie of Irvine won the contract for an initial batch of twelve pump ladder bodies. In turn they engaged their award-winning designer Dawson Sellar, to produce a stylish steel-framed GRP crew cab that neatly married the Leyland "C40" tilt-cab to their aluminium bodywork.

Altogether, 73 Leyland pumps of this type were purchased over a ten-year period. However, competition and complications, including the demise of both Leyland Vehicles and Fulton & Wylie, saw various other companies becoming involved in the construction of both cabs and rear bodies. These suppliers included Emergency One, Lancashire County Council, Mountain Range, and Reynolds Boughton. Another Lancashire coachbuilder, Foster's Commercials Ltd. of Preston, who had supplied some of the pods, became a full-size fire engine builder with a batch of five stunning "Incident Support Units" (emergency tenders) in 1993.

In 1996 the brigade moved forward yet again with its "concept" appliance. In an exciting development, John Taylor persuaded a Dutch fire engine and airfield crash tender builder, Plastisol, to produce a fire appliance to British standards. This had its water and foam tanks moulded integrally into the GRP body! European style such as this would in turn bring major advantages in stowage, overall weight and stability. In a three-way arrangement, a Leyland-based company TVAC *(The Vehicle Application Centre)* was appointed as agent for Plastisol to work with the re-formed Leyland DAF organisation in adapting their new 55 series chassis for the role. Lancashire Fire and Rescue Service have, quite justifiably, dubbed this new vehicle as *"the fire engine of the future."*

Merseyside (1974 to Date)

The new metropolitan county centred on Liverpool and the Wirral towns, could only be called Merseyside, although the inclusion of Southport and St. Helens did stretch the name's riparian associations somewhat. Bootle, Birkenhead and Wallasey, together with elements of the Cheshire and Lancashire brigades completed the picture as the new Metropolitan County Council took over fire protection in an area that was both densely urbanised in some parts, whilst at the same time being very rural in others.

The city fleet was predominantly Dennis and all the other brigades, with the exception of Lancashire, contributed more of the same, though in St. Helens the line-up was principally Leyland. From the outset, the most fascinating segment of the Merseyside fleet has been the aerial appliances, which included a combined contingent of eight AEC/Merryweather TLs. These were joined by the only remaining Morris-Magirus ladder in these parts (Bootle), England's oldest Simon Snorkel and its sister (Liverpool), five 50ft pump-hydraulic platforms (including Southport's) and one Simonitor. Additionally the brigade inherited, via Bootle and St. Helens, the only two Carmichael-Wibe Orbitor platforms ever to serve in the North West.

Like its predecessor, the new authority also provided cover for Speke airport, absorbing the existing Thornycroft fleet. Within a year the brigade acquired an impressive 37-ton Chubb Pathfinder crash tender (in bright yellow), but in 1982 relinquished the airport brigade function.

One of the first new deliveries was the futuristic Chubb "Pacesetter" in 1975, a concept appliance based on the rear-engined Reynolds Boughton Scorpio chassis; Merseyside being the only UK local authority brigade to purchase one. Seven ERF pumps followed and in 1978, a batch of 20 Dennis R133 water ladders, which included the 100th example of this successful model. To mark this, the vehicle was given a special paint finish, chromium plating and a cherished "100" registration. Being posted to Southport the appliance had to have a name, so in honour of the thrice-winning Grand National celebrity that will be forever linked with the town, the new Dennis was appropriately christened *Red Rum*.

Top Left: *A "rum" occasion at Southport fire station as the famous racehorse assists with the naming ceremony of new water ladder* Red Rum *in February 1978. This 100th Dennis R-series appliance (NTJ 100S) incorporated a number of special features.* Beryl McCain

Centre Left: *Among the first replacements for the Liverpool articulated appliances (see chapter eight) were this 1982 Ford D0907 hose layer (XKB 926W) and ex-Birkenhead Commer/Sun foam tender (PCM 662) from 1963, which became a marine fire unit. Both are seen in the "cavernous" engine house at Bankhall (no pun intended on the city's famous Cavern Club of Beatles legend!).*

Bottom Left: *One of three smart-looking Dennis RS133 control unit/emergency tenders bought by Merseyside Fire Brigade, DWM 606Y entered service at the Millfields (St. Helens) station in 1983.* Alastair Collins

In an unusual naming ceremony in February 1978, the four-legged and four-wheeled namesakes met at the Manchester Road fire station in the presence of various dignitaries! Subsequent Southport pumps have proudly perpetuated the *Red Rum* name.

A further ten Dennis R-series were delivered, before the brigade changed to the newer Dennis RS model of which a large number were operated. Three emergency tender/control units were also constructed on Dennis RS133 chassis between 1979 and 1983, but these still incorporated the familiar square steel cab. Around the same time, the brigade replaced its ex-Liverpool fleet of articulated specials with a variety of rigid vehicles performing the same functions, such as hose layer and marine units.

The 1980s were notable for the large-scale replacement of the aerial fleet, principally by "re-chassising" much of the original stock. Merseyside was the most prolific exponent of this practice in the region, with five Merryweather ladders and two 65ft Simon Snorkels being refitted to new Dennis F125 chassis between 1981 and 1985.

A new Dennis/Simon SS263 (91ft) platform was purchased in the same period along with two new turntable ladders, although these were less successful. One of these, on a Dennis DF133 chassis, was the abortive XRL30 electro-hydraulic, intended as Merryweather's comeback model but turning out to be the final 'nail in the coffin' for the ailing manufacturer. The other "new" ladder, mounted on a Dennis F127, was a rare, French-built Camiva 30-metre unit, formerly used as a manufacturer's demonstrator. Each saw a brief stretch of service at Canning Place but, since that time, the brigade has built up a fleet of six Angloco-Bronto aerial ladder platforms (known in the Merseyside Fire Brigade as combined platform ladders) on three-axle Volvo FL10 chassis; these being the only type of aerial currently in service.

The remainder of the special appliance fleet in Merseyside is now catered for by means of demountable bodies, whereby basic chassis serve a variety of different functions through their capacity to mount or demount pods (or bodies) as the situation warrants. A sizeable collection of "pods" has been built up and these fulfil the special rescue, bulk foam, damage control and other roles, being carried on Dennis DFS/Multilift prime movers. Most, though not all, of this equipment is kept at the Kirkdale (Bankhall) station, once the home of the famous artic appliances, meaning that the body-swap concept, originating in Merseyside, has effectively turned a full circle.

Top Right: *One of several "re-chassised" aerials in the Merseyside fleet, this Dennis F125 (A48 HKC) of 1983 carries the 65ft Simon booms from the original Liverpool Snorkel built in 1963 (9750 KF).* Tony Kent

Centre Right: *An unusual appliance was this former demonstrator, a Dennis F127 with John Dennis body and French Camiva turntable ladder, originally built in 1984. It is seen in the station yard at Bankhall, along with a special rescue unit pod built by Bence on the Multilift system.*

Bottom Right: *One of the later Merseyside appliances, T659 CCK is a 1999 Dennis Sabre with bodywork by Emergency One. It is pictured here in service at Kirkby.* Tony Kent

Greater Manchester (1974 To Date)

Above: *Posing for a publicity picture alongside the brigade's preserved Shand Mason horse-drawn 'steamer', shortly after entering service at Bolton in 1979, is the first of the new Dennis RS range (ANC 778T). GMC would ultimately operate 56 similar appliances.*
J.M.Birchall for Bolton Evening News

Another of the five new fire authorities in 1974, Greater Manchester was probably the most complex. With eight county boroughs joining parts of Cheshire and Lancashire county brigades, the priority was to unite these resources into one cohesive organisation. The County Fire Officer and several senior staff came from Lancashire and in order to quickly establish uniform working practices, the new brigade adopted many of the systems and procedures from that authority. However, such unification was not so easily achieved with the rolling stock.

The 1974 fleet of over 150 appliances was a mixture of AEC, Albion, Austin, Bedford, Commer, Dennis, ERF, Ford, Land Rover, Leyland, and Range Rover, with examples of all the well-known (and quite a few of the lesser-known) bodybuilders. The oldest appliance in operational service was Bolton's Commer pump salvage tender dating from 1951, but the brigade also found itself with a 1940 Dennis pump escape still in use at Manchester's London Road training school. This was sold off almost immediately but, nine years later came back as an exhibit in the Brigade Museum.

The ex-Lancashire stock had included many of their more recent and specialised vehicles such as two 3-axle Range Rovers and an experimental articulated emergency tender. This demountable concept was taken up by the new brigade which re-designated the trailer "Operational Support Unit" and followed it up with two control units, a chemical decontamination unit and a canteen van, all based on semi-trailers with Scammell automatic couplings.

Some new appliances were already in the pipeline. A Dennis F48 emergency tender, delivered to Oldham Fire Brigade shortly before changeover, never entered service in the town and was instead sent to London Road, Manchester, as a replacement for a twelve-year-old Leyland Firemaster. Similarly, Manchester's new ERF/Simon "Simonitor," was only weeks old and still being fitted out.

Top Right: *New to Lancashire County just prior to the 1974 reorganisation, this 6-wheel Range Rover with Carmichael Commando rescue tender bodywork (PTJ 699M) was based at Heywood station beside the M62. It saw considerable action as a first-response unit on Greater Manchester's motorways for ten years until replaced by a Land Rover 110.* GMFS Museum

Centre Right: *Between 1976 and 1978 GMC Fire Service achieved early standardisation with the purchase of over 50 identical water ladders. Based on Ford D1617 chassis with "no-frills" HCB-Angus bodies, they proved to be tough workhorses. This example, OVU 859R of 1976, was posted to Stalybridge.*

Bottom Right: *The brigade operated a fleet of articulated special appliances for several years, along with a number of Ford and Dodge tractor units. One of these, a Ford tractor unit (GFR 218N), based at Agecroft station, is seen with one of the brigade's two control unit trailers at a fire in Salford in 1977.*

A water tender and an HCB-Angus/Simon SS220 hydraulic platform, both on ERF chassis, were delivered after a few months but it was the brigade's desire to standardise the appliances as soon as possible. Although ambitious, this plan was achieved in an impressive timescale. Lancashire had only bought Ford pumping appliances since 1970 and this make was also chosen for Greater Manchester's new water tender fleet. The 16-ton D1617 chassis with the Perkins engine was selected and a sizeable order placed with HCB-Angus for the bodywork. The specification included 1000-gpm Godiva pumps and 45ft alloy extension ladders.

The first of the new appliances (MND 712P) entered service at Agecroft fire station, Pendlebury in March 1976. Within two years, the brigade had placed no less than 53 identical Fords in service at stations throughout the county, including the bastions of more "quality" products, such as Bolton (AEC), Stockport (ERF) and Salford (Dennis). The sight of two mass-produced "county-style" water tenders with fluorescent red cabs, unpainted aluminium bodywork and ***no wheeled escapes*** in the engine house at Manchester's London Road station, saddened the heart of many a traditionalist during this honeymoon period.

By the late 1970s, the brigade was considering its next generation of water tenders and, after several accidents, placed fire-fighter safety at the top of its list of requirements. A crash-proof steel cab was a must, along with Manchester-style rear-facing crew seats. However, the existing safety-cab appliances on the market were Bedford-based and unable to meet the engine specifications for Greater Manchester's 1000-gpm pumps.

The brigade therefore entered into dialogue with Dennis, who were then developing a steel safety cab of their own in conjunction with Ogle Design Ltd. As a result, the prototype of the new Dennis RS series and a sister appliance entered service at Bolton in August 1979, to be followed by over 50 more for the brigade within five years. Despite a universal corrosion problem, the RS was a winning formula with an excellent safety record. This author undoubtedly owes his life to the quality and strength of a Dennis RS cab in a 1984 accident.

Despite the standardised pumping fleet, GMC's special appliances were more varied. The aerial fleet at this stage consisted of ERF and Shelvoke, whilst Ford and Dodge chassis were used for foam tenders, emergency tenders and the like, with various bodybuilders such as Eagle, Cheshire Fire Engineering and Angloco all finding favour. Cheshire bodybuilder Mountain Range of Crewe, which had already supplied two rescue tenders and two emergency salvage tenders to the brigade, won a 1984 contract for eleven water tenders based on the Dodge G13C.

The fleet became predominantly Dodge for the next few years with five "low-cab" hydraulic platforms, seven Magirus turntables, and over 60 more pumping appliances split between Mountain Range and Fulton & Wylie of Irvine. *(For non-North West readers wondering where the mountainous part of Cheshire lies, the firm took its name from proprietor Ron Mountain).*

As well as Dodge chassis, the brigade has operated Leyland appliances, beginning with a single water tender on Freighter chassis in 1987. Further Freighters (the more recent ones badged as Leyland-DAF) and half a dozen Roadrunner-based emergency salvage tenders summarise the main contribution by the Lancashire manufacturer. The latter were built to a uniform design by several smaller firms, including Nova Scotia and Bedwas, and intended principally for urban use. With their heavy duty cutting, lighting and "mopping-up" equipment, the lightweight Roadrunners have found themselves pounding the Greater Manchester motorways, including the notorious "Rockingstones" high-altitude stretch of the Trans-Pennine M62, ever since the demise of the "light rescue vehicle" concept.

The year 1992 saw the first of many Volvo machines for Greater Manchester, in the guise of a 3-axle FL10 fitted with prototype Simon ST290S (29-metre) aerial ladder platform (ALP), one of seven. Two years later, after brief flings with both the Renault Midliner and the Dennis DF, the brigade began an enduring affair with the Volvo Marque. Furthermore, nowadays Greater Manchester has returned to its "standard pumping appliance" policy, commendably embarked upon over 25 years earlier, despite some interesting diversions along the way.

Since 1983, GMC Fire Service has operated a successful museum at Rochdale fire station. Conceived, designed and cared for by serving or retired members of the brigade, the museum houses over a dozen historic fire appliances dating from as far back as 1741. Uniforms, equipment, photographs, models and archive material can also be seen. For further details regarding open days or group visits, readers can contact the museum on **01706 900155**.

Top Left: *As well as a large fleet of Dodge water tenders, GMC also operated this neat-looking Carmichael foam tender on the G13C chassis. Based at Sale, it was well placed to attend a large petrochemical plant and several major risks on the Trafford Park industrial estate.* Alan Gartside

Bottom Left: *The 29-metre ST290S aerial ladder platform was specially developed by Simon for the Greater Manchester brigade. The first of seven, on 6x4 Volvo FL10 chassis (J561 PND), was delivered in 1992 and is pictured at the Salford Quays development, built on the city's former docklands.* GMC Fire Service

Cheshire (1974 To Date)

The present Cheshire brigade still retains much of its pre-1974 shape, size and operating methods, despite losing some stations to Greater Manchester and Merseyside that year. Gains included the former Chester city brigade also the towns of Widnes and Warrington, from across the Manchester Ship Canal. Like Chester, Warrington had its own fire brigade and is now one of the busiest stations in the authority. The existing Cheshire fleet, largely Dennis and ERF, was in pretty good shape on reorganisation. Not surprisingly, appliances of these makes acquired from Warrington and Chester fitted easily into the larger picture, even if the same could not be said for Warrington's remaining two Bedford machines, nor the pair of ex-Lancashire Fords at Widnes.

New deliveries commenced in 1974 with an all-ERF water ladder for Chester. The same station received a new Dennis F49 emergency tender the following year, a welcome replacement for the old "accident unit", an ex-Civil Defence soft-top Land-Rover. The tradition of full-size emergency tenders in the region was kept alive by Cheshire who bought two more Dennis examples, for Widnes and Crewe, before the decade was over.

An early purchase was yet another Simon 50ft pump-hydraulic platform for the North West, based on a Rolls-Royce powered ERF. The county's continuing allegiance to Dennis products was demonstrated with a batch of nine R-series water tenders in 1978, two being modified to a lower height to fit older stations at Nantwich and Stockton Heath.

To cope with the county's not inconsiderable industrial risk, now increased by the inclusion of Widnes and Warrington, a number of Dennis special appliances were purchased. These included two Dennis Delta II foam tenders for Warrington and Ellesmere Port in 1978. Two years later came a pair of Dennis-Simon SS263 (91ft) hydraulic platforms on the F125 Delta chassis that went to Chester and Macclesfield. A solitary Dennis DF133 turntable ladder, with Carmichael-Magirus equipment, also appeared at Warrington in 1984. This part of the county has seen massive development in recent years, with the construction of Warrington and Birchwood "new towns" and the building of the east-west M62 motorway, which crosses the M6 at the notorious Croft interchange.

Top Right: *This 1978 Dennis R-series water ladder (VCA 494R) was specially modified to fit inside the low roofed engine house at Cheshire's Nantwich fire station.* Tony Kent

Centre Right: *One of two light rescue tenders built by Macclesfield Motor Bodies Ltd. on the American GMC K30 chassis (F368 KTU) poses beside the M6 motorway in Cheshire with its lighting mast extended. The pair was followed by two similar appliances, bodied by Jennings, and all four were later converted to hazardous materials units by MMB.* Macclesfield Motor Bodies Ltd

Bottom Right: *The second Locomotors-built fire engine to serve the town of Macclesfield in 60 years was K632 KMB, part of Cheshire's original 1992 batch of Mercedes 1124F water ladders, and the only one with a white-painted bumper.* Gavin Stewart

A brace of 3-axle Range Rover/Carmichael rescue tenders was commissioned in 1978 and stationed at Birchwood and Knutsford for motorway service. Further light special appliances were purchased over the next few years, some based on the Ford A-series that was enjoying popularity at the time. The Land Rover pumping fleet was also renewed, whilst another interesting lightweight appliance consisted of a four-wheel-drive Bedford CF van, modified by the brigade in 1982 to cover the out-of-town "Shopping City" near Runcorn.

The 1980s saw a mixed bag of new Dennis pumps, including steel-cabbed RS133s, the narrower DS and some tilt-cab SS models. Six SS135 water tenders bought in 1987 were built by Excalibur CBK of Stoke-on-Trent, the first this company had built on the Dennis chassis. Two years later, the brigade acquired two rescue tenders based on the unusual General Motors K30 4x4. These were built in Cheshire by Macclesfield Motor Bodies (UK) Ltd., nowadays better known for its ambulances. Two further K30s, and a Carmichael-Bronto aerial ladder platform on Scania chassis, highlighted the fact that Britain's vehicle manufacturing base was shrinking, but a 1992 batch of 14 water tenders on Mercedes chassis represented a major departure from tradition.

The bodybuilder, Locomotors of Hampshire, was a relative newcomer to mainstream fire-engine manufacture, or so it seemed. In fact the company, part of the Rank-Hovis-McDougall organisation, had a long history of commercial vehicle manufacture, once having a factory in Macclesfield that built at least one fire engine in the 1930s.

Another six Mercedes pumps, with Carmichael bodies, came in 1994, but more recent purchases have been mainly Dennis Sabre, with bodies by John Dennis Coachbuilders. This supplier was also responsible for two impressive foam tenders supplied in 1997 for service in Ellesmere Port and Warrington, as replacements for the earlier Dennis Deltas. The new vehicles were based on the 26-tonne, 6-wheel ERF EC8 chassis, with rear-steer axle and featured 11,000-litre Kenilworth bulk tanks.

Acknowledgements

In the century covered by this publication, the region's fire appliances have changed beyond recognition. Many of the famous manufacturing names have disappeared completely whilst some, like Leyland, have been "reborn" and can still be found today.

Meanwhile, the fire brigades themselves, having undergone many organisational changes somehow continue to retain the distinctive character and traditions of the North West. The future shape of Britain's fire services is still to be determined, but it is not beyond the imagination to one day envisage a single fire authority serving the whole of the region.

I hope this book has provided an insight into the fascinating subject of North West fire engines through the years and would like to thank the many people, fire authorities and companies who have helped me in its preparation. In addition to those whose names appear under illustrations, I would particularly acknowledge the assistance of the following:

Cheshire Fire Service
(SDO Geoff Hayes)
Cumbria Fire Service
(Sub Officer Phil Chalmers)
Greater Manchester County Fire Service,
Lancashire Fire & Rescue Service
(John Taylor)
Merseyside Fire Service,
North West Evening Mail
(Bill Myers and Heather Horner)
Andy Bentley, Geoff Bottomley,
Roy Breese, Percy Duff,
Aidan Fisher, Graham Hibbert,
Barry Martin, David Plant,
David Spicer, and Neil Steele.

Left: *When ERF Ltd celebrated the move from the famous "Sun Works" factory Sandbach (to a new site in Middlewich) in August 2000, two members of the Cheshire fleet took part in the historic procession of over 100 vehicles. Seen here is P135 RMA, a 1997 EC8/John Dennis foam tender based at Warrington. The other was the latest ERF EC8 hydraulic platform from Macclesfield, a re-chassised 91ft Simon built in 1999.*